simple

small groups

A User-Friendly Guide for Small Group Leaders

BILL SEARCH

BakerBooks

a division of Baker Publishing Group
Grand Rapids, Michigan

To my wife, Karyn.
It's hard to explain something so wonderful . . .

© 2008 by Bill Search

Published by Baker Books
a division of Baker Publishing Group
P.O. Box 6287, Grand Rapids, MI 49516–6287
www.bakerbooks.com

Printed in the United States of America

Library of Congress Cataloging-in-Publication Data
Search, Bill, 1971–
      Simple small groups : a user-friendly guide for small group leaders / Bill
Search.
          p.   cm.
      Includes bibliographical references (p.   ).
      ISBN 978-0-8010-7153-9 (pbk.)
      1. Church group work. 2. Small groups—Religious aspects—Christianity.
I. Title.
BV652.2.S42 2008
253'.7—dc22   2008024788

contents

3

foreword

I have been more than encouraged by the rediscovery of communal life in churches that transcends Sunday services and official gatherings. The group life movement in recent decades is evidence of this return. As a result, a variety of models and strategies have evolved to guide people to a place—a small group—where, as Parker Palmer says, "obedience to truth can be practiced." This has been a wonderful development.

But some approaches to group life in the church felt wooden and forced, placing institutional goals ahead of group health. It became more important to be in a group than to become a community. Leaders were judged by the size of their groups, the number of baptisms, study guides completed, problems avoided, or lost people invited. What began as a desire to connect people to community became a program—a rigid, lifeless system of rules, meetings, guidelines, and objectives. I should know. I have seen many of these. And unfortunately I have contributed to the problem myself at times.

Thankfully, a number of voices have emerged to call us back to the core. Voices that ask real questions: Why are we here? What is real community? What does it mean to be a grace-giving, Christ-loving collection of followers eager to support one another and rescue those who have strayed from the God who loves them?

Bill Search is one of these voices. In *Simple Small Groups* Bill calls us back to what got us here—a simpler journey into meaningful communal life that transforms followers and dispenses grace to those who wander. His candor, experience, and passion will cause the reader to ask one penetrating question: what are we becoming together, and for what mission are we giving our lives when we gather as a group? It is the question of a lifetime, and Bill not only raises it but offers some practical (but not simplistic) insights for group leaders like you and me to turn our missional vision into reality.

I hope that Bill's voice stirs the voice that speaks inside you—that still, small voice of the Spirit guiding you to a simpler life in community so that you are prepared to engage the challenges of a fragmented and complex world.

Dr. Bill Donahue
Executive Director of Group Life,
Willow Creek Association

acknowledgments

A good book on small groups must be written in community, not isolation. God has given me good communities and good friends who have influenced this work through the years, and I can't possibly thank all the many people whom God has used to shape my understanding not only of small groups ministry but of the Christian life. So please forgive me if your name is missing from the extensive list below, but know that I appreciate you nonetheless.

My most important community: My wife, Karyn, and our kids. I am so grateful to my beautiful, brilliant, godly wife who endured through this with me. You encouraged, supported, and bore the lion's share of family life while I escaped to Starbucks to write. Maggie, Emma, and Jack—thanks for your patience while Daddy sat at the dining table with earphones in, editing and editing and editing . . .

My staff: Nevan Hooker, Jon Weiner, Susan St. Clair, Ross Brodfuehrer, Jerry Naville, Rich Shanks, Jenny Brown, and Jennifer Ballengee. You pushed, questioned, and helped me better understand what I was trying to say. A special thanks to Jenny and Michael Brown, who found the right word, cultivate, to explain the missional "C." Special thanks to Nevan Hooker for your dedicated, creative support for all things *Simple Small Groups*. Many thanks to Don Waddell for providing great questions and challenging thoughts to improve the manuscript.

My church: Thanks to Dave Stone, my senior minister and enthusiastic champion for groups along with Brett DeYoung. It is truly a privilege to serve with you both. I must also thank the small group (and big group) leaders at Southeast Christian Church who quickly embraced us almost two years ago and made us feel at home.

My spiritual family: Kent Odor—you really are my Obi Wan Kenobi. God brought your wisdom, guidance, and encouragement to me at exactly the right time. And, thanks to Brett Eastman for introducing me to Kent! Bill Willits—you are part coach, part cheerleader, and part role model. Joe Myers—your questions and ideas have propelled me into deeper thinking about the whole small group movement. Bill Donahue, Greg Bowman, Russ Robinson, Dave Treat, and Steve Gladden—you guys are a gift to the church and have taught me so much about this ministry. Anne Wagner—you have consistently challenged me both personally and professionally to aim higher and allow God to direct my course.

My groups: Cary, Daryl, and Dave—I look forward to our journey together. Josh and Doug—because of you I know what groups can be, and I know that there are bonds of brotherhood stronger than flesh and blood.

My heritage: Jeff Manion—thank you for bringing me back to church ministry all those years ago. I am grateful for my Ada Bible Church family, who provided the fertile soil for many concepts in this book and who allowed God to develop in me a love for groups ministry. Thanks to the groups team at Ada—Phil, Iva, Jim, Kevin, Mike, and Bob— with whom I was privileged to have learned and grown by serving so many great group leaders.

My parents: Mom and Dad—thanks for pushing and prodding me all those years ago. Mom and Dad Wallace, thanks for your constant encouragement and support.

And finally, thanks to my editor, Chad Allen. You transformed ramblings into coherent thoughts. Now I know what concrete means! It's been a pleasure working with you.

introduction

Confessions of a Small Groups Minister

I am an unlikely small groups minister.

In fact, twelve years ago I was a small groups skeptic.

As the early wave of small group fervor was just hitting churches, I wasn't even sure what a small group was, but I was pretty sure I didn't want to be in one. Besides the obvious scariness of being in a confined space with church people, the whole thing seemed like a blind date that everyone expected to be a marriage. Then there were the terms small groups people threw around: discipleship, community, facilitating, *birthing*! It's no wonder I ran in the other direction!

When my wife, Karyn, finally convinced me to go, I didn't know who the small group leader was, but I was sure, with my bachelor's degree in Bible and theology and my master's in educational ministries, that I was bound to be sharper than whoever they put in front of me. And here he was: a twentysomething, Brian, with a big grin and a Bible. *Oh boy*, I thought, *here we go*.

Like I said, it was Karyn's idea. We had met with the small groups pastor, Steve, and he talked with us about groups and where he thought we could plug in. I kept trying to put the whole thing off, but we had just gotten married, and Karyn was desperate for a place to belong as a couple.

So I bit the bullet . . . and signed up for leadership training. If I was going to be in a group, I reasoned, I would lead the thing. Unfortunately, "leadership training" was more like "leadership torment." It involved several hours of watching videotapes of some ancient small group expert. I made it through exactly one hour of "training," gave up, and Karyn and I joined a group.

It felt like defeat.

To make matters worse, the first night we were to meet with our new group, Karyn didn't feel well, conveniently, but asked me to go and represent the team.

"But I won't know anybody!" I protested.

"Bill, you can do it. I don't want them to think we're flaking out already."

"Yeah, but . . ."

"Bill. Please?"

Fifteen minutes later I grudgingly pulled into the small group host's driveway. The living room was full of five eager couples and me. Our leader, Brian, led off with a get-to-know-you ice breaker: "If you were a cartoon character, who would you be?"

Lord, I prayed, *could we have that rapture thing now, please?!*

The worst part was when one of the other guys in the group, Scott, told the group who he would be. I don't remember what he said, but it was absolutely hilarious. The group guffawed. *Oh no*, I thought, *my job as group comedian just got taken!* I consoled myself with the notion that I would be the "Bible school graduate" of the group. Then we came to Travis and Patty. As they introduced themselves, they told the breathtaking story of how they met on the mission field in Kenya. Ugh. Two missionaries trump a Bible school graduate, easy.

10

Shoot, I wondered, *what on earth will they think of me?*
To make a long story short, my wife did come to the next
meeting. And then we went to a third meeting. And a fourth.
And so on, until slowly the group felt less and less like an
obligation. I learned I didn't have to play a role. I could just be
myself. The group eventually became a gathering of friends
who supported and challenged each other to be better followers of Jesus. We studied the Bible, talked about it, and
applied it to our lives. I'm not certain when it occurred, but
our small group became life changing for me.

Strange as it was, I looked forward to group.

Our Need for Community

That was twelve years ago, and since then I have been involved in a number of small groups. I've been a participant
and a leader. I've been in couples groups, men's groups,
short-term groups, longer groups—I've even sat in a women's
group! But after all these years one thing is very clear to me:
All of us need an authentic community.

God wired us to require others. God said, "Let us make
man in our image" (Gen. 1:26). The "us" and "our" of that
statement is not God talking with the angels; it's God talking
to the other members of the Trinity. (So next time someone
asks why you're talking to yourself, tell them you're reflecting God's image!) After he made the first person he said, "It
is not good . . ."

What's strange is that this is the first time God called
something "not good." At this point in the narrative, God has
created a perfect world, without flaw or sin. The first person
was perfect, had work, and an unhindered relationship with
God. But it was "not good" for man to be alone.

The truth is we need people. Blaise Pascal said we were
created with a "God-shaped void." In other words, we crave
God, and if we don't have him, we settle for a cheap substitute.

11

Others have said God also created us with a person-shaped void; and again if it is not completed in community, we will seek cheap substitutes.

Adam needed company. He needed friendship. He had God, but that was not enough. Sounds like heresy when I say it. But God said it first. We need him. But we need other people too.

Things Get Complicated

This need for community[1] wound its way throughout history. The community of believers has gone by different names, and most recently the phenomenon has emerged as small groups. In the next chapter I'll address the history of small groups, but what's important for us to recognize here is that over the years, small groups have become complicated. When I led my first group I struggled with all sorts of doubts. What is a group supposed to be? Is it primarily an in-depth Bible study? Is it a social club for the relationally unattached? Is it a support and encouragement group? Is it for people who serve together? Is it best to gather people who are like each other? Or is it better to form groups in neighborhoods? Is a group supposed to encourage believers? Or is it supposed to evangelistically reach out? Do groups have a mandate to fully disciple the member? Or does the rest of the church have a role in that too? Perhaps, like me, you wistfully shrug and wonder what your group is supposed to accomplish.

If a leader is perusing the small groups section of a Christian bookstore, they will find books that espouse different and sometimes contradictory positions in relation to the above questions. If a group leader or a small group pastor isn't aware of the different approaches to groups, they will likely be confused by the sheer volume and variety of small group philosophies.

I recall a meeting with several small group ministers a few years ago. We sat around a large table. On the opposite side of a bank of windows, a whiteboard covered the wall. We were each sharing what was working for our ministries and what was not working. Rob stood up and said, "Well, we used to know that groups were best formed by gathering people who were similar. We now know that the best groups are formed of people who live near each other." At first I thought he was being facetious. He was not. He was shifting from one philosophy of how you do groups to another. Rob's a smart guy and knew he was making a shift. There are several different small group philosophies that confuse full-time small group ministers. My heart bleeds for the leader who might become overwhelmed by the options.

Over the years that I've been in small groups, I've seen models come and go—from intensive discipleship to special interest groups for bicyclists and quilters, to groups that do nothing but read large portions of the Bible together, to groups that are geographically connected somehow. It leads me to ask, Is a new model of groups really the answer? That's where simple small groups isn't really a model. It's merely a way of making whatever model you like best work better.

As we explore simple small groups we need to honestly assess the different motives that drive some churches to implement small groups. Some hope to develop deep, spiritual community. But some churches have ulterior motives and a leader, at some point, will pick up this. Some churches want groups to be their only form of discipleship. As a small group leader you may feel the pressure to take a person from seeker to missionary in two years in a small group that meets every other week. While groups are an essential piece of the discipleship process, you need the support of the whole church to fully develop a person spiritually.[2]

In some churches groups are also expected to help retain attenders. Church strategy experts call this "closing the back door." The assumption is that if people relationally

13

connect with a handful of other people, they are less likely to leave the church. While this might be effective for a time, churches that look to groups to keep people from leaving might want to look at the other reasons they are leaving. When a leader begins to feel that their group is really a retention strategy for the church it cheapens the real value of biblical community.

In other churches, groups are expected to be the missional arm of the church. In such churches leaders and group members are contacted constantly to serve, give, donate, and evangelize. Since group members are often the core of the church, this faithful group gets tapped for more and more. But as a leader you know the pressure this puts on a group of people who are likely already serving and giving. In one group I was part of, the leader told us that one of the pastors asked him to ask the group for volunteers for a program. This was not the first time our group members were asked to volunteer. Without hesitating Susie barked back, "If the pastor was doing his job he wouldn't have to keep asking us for help!" Her response demonstrated how hard it is for leaders to both serve their group and serve as an agent of the church. Expecting groups to be missional is even more challenging in a church with little concern for those outside the faith. Such a church is not likely to promote groups that have this passion.

It's crazy the problems we expect groups to fix! If the local church itself has a problem, chances are the groups within that church will have the same problem. If the church has a problem growing believers, groups will have a problem too. If the local church has no sense of community and connection, chances are the groups won't fix that. If there is no missional pulse for reaching out to the people outside the church, the group will likely resemble the club that the local church has grown into. Just like a dysfunctional, troubled family might pass on dysfunction and trouble to the children, an unhealthy church will often have groups that are similarly unhealthy.

Three Simple Patterns

If you are a small group leader reading this book, chances are you know exactly what I'm talking about. You are attempting to build community and help people grow, and the pastor emails you with new duties and expectations. You agreed to open up your home and your heart, and now you have a checklist of other responsibilities. The picture of the church in the second chapter of Acts captured you, and you wanted to feel a sense of family with some other followers of Christ; now you are feeling like a cog in the wheel of a giant strategy.

Over the last few years as a small groups pastor I've been on a personal quest to identify and then explain simple patterns for small groups. My goal is for a small group leader, coach, member, or pastor to be able to remember what a group is. This book is not concerned with how groups are formed or coached, if they are comprised of believers or seekers or both. Strategies and methods change. In just the last ten years I've watched trends in group life come and go. My hope is that by the end of this book you will have a more solid understanding of what makes a healthy group.

While groups can try to accomplish a laundry list of duties, in my experience groups can expect to do just a few things well. Being a Michigan native I've maintained an on-again, off-again love of the Detroit Tigers. Throughout most of their history they've been a decent team. But from time to time they have been champions. In 2006 a seemingly unlikely thing happened. An old manager with a team of young, nameless players won the pennant. When manager Jim Leyland took over the Tigers, they were one of the worst teams in Major League Baseball. Winning the American

League Pennant that year was nothing short of a miracle. Countless times Leyland was asked how he turned the Tigers around. He didn't offer complicated answers; he simply pointed out that he focused the team on the basics.[3] From baseball to small groups, when we focus on the basics we do well. I'm no baseball expert, but when it comes to groups, the three *simple* patterns that lead to a healthy small group are connecting, changing, and cultivating.

Connecting is the growing sense of connection with an identified group of people. My friend Joe Myers explains in his book *The Search to Belong* that we need different "spaces" of connection. For a group, community is with select people who meet regularly. They may start as casual acquaintances, but some will become friends and perhaps even a family. We can't promise every group will experience deep intimacy. But intimacy isn't required for group members to experience connecting. I'll say more on this later.

Changing is the spiritual and relational renovation that transforms us into the likeness of Christ. It is not merely intellectual; it is not behavior modification. It happens when we take on the character and mind of Christ. In a small group, change usually comes as someone holds up the mirror and encourages us to look at ourselves without a filter. Are we really becoming the person Jesus wants us to become?

Cultivating is the missional lifestyle. It's not only evangelism or only service. It's both. When a group is cultivating, they are developing an outward focus that engages their hearts into action. We become aware of the needs of others and want to pitch in. A group helps us remember that every follower of Christ is called to make an impact on the world around us and to build God's kingdom. A group helps us explore our spiritual gifts and encourages us to live a missional life. This isn't about obligation and feelings of guilt—when a group cultivates missional lives they look forward to involvement.

I would like to suggest that we explore these three Cs as "patterns," not "laws" or "rules," of small groups. They describe healthy groups, how they function, and why some groups struggle. While more patterns could be added, I would argue that the more activities and expectations groups try to add, the more difficult it will be to achieve health. Besides, as Russ Robinson, author and former small group champion at Willow Creek, has often said, "Groups can accomplish only three things. If you add anything else they will treat it like a menu and choose the three things they want to do."[4] Perhaps you have read off the menu, and like Russ predicted, you chose your options.

I will also talk about "harmony" between the three patterns, not "balance" or "equality." A transformational small group might focus 80 percent of its time on community development and split the rest between change and cultivating. This is not a problem. Many great communities in the Scriptures could be described as "unbalanced." They didn't always try to keep things even. At times they needed to pray for hours. And at other times they needed to spend time in the community. The goal is harmony—the inclusion of all three patterns in the group.

Originally, I wanted to call this book *It Seemed Like a Good Idea at the Time: Confessions of a "Successful" Small Groups Pastor*. Through the years I have enjoyed working in growing ministries and with great small groups teams. We have tried nearly every new trend that has come our way. Many of them have worked. We have increased the number of groups, the retention of leaders, and the satisfaction of people in those groups. But with each "success" we were plagued with one question: What defines a healthy small group? Most of the energy has been spent on strategy and implementation without definition. The purpose of this book is to describe the simple patterns that make for a healthy group.

I hope the book stirs your thinking. I hope it's helpful as you identify where a group experience has been healthy. Sometimes things go well and we don't know why. Perhaps after reading *Simple Small Groups* you'll have a better understanding of those good experiences. Other times things go terribly, and we're mystified. I hope this book will help you better understand these situations as well.

Thanks for exploring these patterns with me.

1

how we got here

Hints from History

We have to be honest: throughout most of church history, small groups as we think of them did not exist. However, small gatherings of believers, meeting in homes, facilitated by a leader, are not a new phenomenon. In the first few hundred years of the church they were not optional. In fact, they were the primary way to experience the church until Christianity was legalized in AD 313.

A First-Century Tale of Simple Community

Travel back with me two thousand years ago to an imaginary couple . . .

Newly married Joshua and Sarah entered the temple courtyard in Jerusalem with a few coins in their purse. The working-class couple was eager to purchase a pair of birds and offer sacrifice to God. But as they approached the vendors to buy a bird, a gathering of people in a corner of the courtyard captured their attention. For reasons they couldn't explain they found themselves wandering over to explore the commotion. Joshua and Sarah stumbled upon a passionate speaker. His clothing quickly indicated that he was not one of the religious leaders. But his talk captivated them. The speaker talked about his rabbi, a man named Jesus, and how Jesus was the Messiah that the prophets said would come. As residents of Jerusalem they knew the name Jesus. They listened on, confused, since they had heard that Jesus had been crucified. They didn't know it, but the speaker was Peter, a close follower of Jesus. But they were less interested in who was speaking than what he was speaking about. He talked about hope in this life and the life after this. He insisted that though Jesus had died, he had returned from the dead to prove his power over death. Peter talked about forgiveness of sin that no longer required an animal sacrifice. Joshua and Sarah were mesmerized.

The name of Jesus was legendary. They knew the stories. They heard he healed people. There were rumors he multiplied a small basket of food into a feast for masses. But they also knew how furious the name of Jesus made the leaders—both religious and Roman. His execution had been just a short time ago. As Peter—and other disciples of Jesus—described the appearance of Jesus after his death a strange thing happened. Joshua and Sarah looked at each other with nodding approval and quietly said to each other, "I believe him." Curiosity morphed into belief. They weren't the only ones. They began to understand that the salvation the prophets talked about wasn't relief from the Romans but deliverance from the burden of sin. They came to the temple to buy two pigeons and instead were given eternal life.

"Now what?" one person in the crowd shouted. "I believe you!" exclaimed another. With raised eyebrows Peter looked at a young, bearded man several feet away. They both smiled and then Peter said, "Follow Christ in baptism. Show that you believe in this act." There was a logistical problem, however;

the crowd had swelled to hundreds and it seemed they all wanted to be baptized.

Led by Peter, the crowd migrated to a nearby pool just outside the temple. In a mass exodus Joshua and Sarah followed Peter from the temple to the pool and there with hundreds of other new believers celebrated their new faith by entering the water. Soaking wet they raced home to tell Joshua's widowed mother the great news. Unfortunately, it was not welcome news. Quite the opposite: Joshua's mother burst into tears and dragged them a couple of blocks away to the synagogue. His sobbing mother pleaded with the leader of the synagogue to explain that Jesus was nothing more than a deranged man with delusions of grandeur. With great command of the Scriptures the teacher complied with the older woman's wishes. He laughed at the notion that Jesus had returned from the grave and suggested that perhaps Jesus's followers had simply stolen the body of their leader.

Joshua and Sarah returned home exhausted and confused. Were they wrong? Were they duped? Or were they right?

Instead of tending to his work the next day, Joshua suggested to Sarah that they return to the temple and try to find Peter or someone who might be able to explain some things to them. Again, they found a crowd gathered around Peter, whose voice was almost hoarse from preaching. Joshua wanted to blurt a simple question: "What should I do with my mom, who thinks we're crazy?" But it didn't seem very appropriate. He estimated that there were about five hundred people crowded around Peter that day. It would have been rude to bark out a question. He figured he would simply hold his question until Peter took a break. As soon as the much-anticipated break came, with Sarah clutching his hand, Joshua lurched toward Peter. But they weren't the only people with questions. It was impossible to draw close enough to ask Peter what to do.

Fortunately, on their way toward the famed apostle, Joshua and Sarah bumped into a kindly, barrel-chested man in his midforties. The fuzzy-faced fellow grinned at them and cheerfully said, "A bit hard to talk with that man, isn't it?" Continuing his smile, he said, "I'm Simeon. You look a little frazzled. Is there anything I can do to help?" It was then they realized that they didn't know what to ask. They described to Simeon how they came to the temple to worship the previous day, were drawn to the crowd, and found that Peter's explanation made sense. Simeon nodded knowingly, smile still on his face, and interjected, "Let me guess: you got baptized, went home, your family didn't share your enthusiasm, and now you want to know what's next?"

"Yeah, that sums it up!" Joshua exclaimed. "We believe, but now what? My mother thinks we're crazy, and the leader of the synagogue thinks we're heretics."

"I know how you feel. Some of us meet in homes after we meet at the temple. It gives us a chance to talk about the sermon and pray for each other. Why don't you come over to my house today? I'm pretty sure Peter's done talking. After all, did you hear his voice? He's going to lose it altogether if he doesn't take a break."

Joshua and Sarah figured it was either that or return to his sobbing mother. They followed Simeon, who was joined by about a dozen other people. From the temple it was about a fifteen-minute walk. As they walked, the small huddle introduced themselves. There were carpenters, a mill operator, two shepherds, one former beggar, and a few shopkeepers. As they arrived at Simeon's home, they entered a modest-sized courtyard flanked by covered rooms on three sides, which all opened to the central space. A few people went into a side room and began to prepare food as the rest lingered on the low couches and got to know each other.

They quickly discovered they had much in common. Each one had wandered into the temple to worship when they were captivated with the Good News that they didn't need to offer animal sacrifice to be forgiven. They had all become followers of Jesus. But they also soon discovered that most of their friends and families weren't keen on the new faith. One man's wife left him, and an older couple was ostracized by their neighbors. But they all shared one more key feature: they wanted to know what to do now. How should they live differently now that they believed that Jesus had died for their sins and was raised from the dead? Ben, a merchant, was the first to suggest it. What if they gathered together each day and talked about how to live like Jesus would want them to live? Everyone instantly agreed. They would meet at the temple, then stroll to Simeon's house.

These meetings became the high point of the day for young Sarah and Joshua. They soon discovered there were twelve apostles, and each one would take turns telling stories about lessons Jesus had taught them. And after each large gathering at the temple, they would head over to Simeon's house for food and conversation. Of course, a large part of the conversation was how to put hands and feet to the teaching they had just heard. On one particular evening Ben was struggling with how to live out "blessed are the meek." As a confident, sometimes cocky, businessman, he worried that if he was meek with potential customers they would not believe his products were better than other merchants'. Would he lose business if he took a more humble approach? The group talked about the implications of what the apostle Matthew called "the Sermon on the Mount." Funny name for a sermon, the group concurred. They ended that evening by praying specifically for Ben that the Holy Spirit would guide him on how to be a meek merchant.

It wasn't only good conversation that kept Simeon's group together. The older couple who had been ostracized by neighbors, Saul and Rachel, were soon ignored by their children as well. This was a real problem for the aged pair, who relied on their grown children for food and support. If they would abandon Jesus, they were told, then their children would continue supporting them. The group rallied around Saul and Rachel. Ben gave them some money. Joshua went to their home and repaired a broken doorway. Sarah brought them food at lunch. It seemed that each member of the group offered them some support.

As the weeks stretched into months, what began as a band of strangers became a family. They shared joys and pains. They celebrated when a friend or family member accepted Jesus as Messiah. What started with thirteen people became twenty-eight! However, some aspects of their group remained the same. They continued to meet in Simeon's house—though now they used each side room and even the roof! They became a closer-knit community than they ever expected. Each day they ate together. Someone always brought flat bread and olive oil. Sometimes they ate soup or vegetables. On rare occasions they would roast a lamb. There was always food. And the topic never changed—whatever the apostles taught that day was the subject that night. They wanted to live out whatever they were taught. Each member of the group wanted to become more like the Jesus who gave them new life.

And the group grew! New faces kept showing up, because a community that loved Jesus and each other welcomes in others in need of Jesus. Joshua, Sarah, Simeon, Ben, Saul, and Rachel remembered what it was like to be alone and wandering and welcomed in people just like they were.

The Biblical Account

This fictional depiction of a first-century small group is actually not far-fetched. Luke writes,

> They devoted themselves to the apostles' teaching and to the fellowship, to the breaking of bread and to prayer. Everyone was filled with awe, and many wonders and miraculous signs were done by the apostles. All the believers were together and had everything in common. Selling their possessions

and goods, they gave to anyone as he had need. Every day they continued to meet together in the temple courts. They broke bread in their homes and ate together with glad and sincere hearts, praising God and enjoying the favor of all the people. And the Lord added to their number daily those who were being saved.

Acts 2:42–47

The people drawn into the message of Jesus found themselves in a new community. For some, their old one rejected them. But for all of them, a new belief led to a new family—a family with new traditions and patterns. As we explore Luke's description of the early church, we can clearly see three simple patterns:

1. A relational pattern: they gathered in homes and shared meals.
2. A growth pattern: they talked about the teachings of Jesus.
3. A missional pattern: they increased.

The Relational Pattern: Connecting

The earliest form of the church was not only dedicated to large public gatherings. They were also devoted to home fellowship. The word *fellowship* was often used to describe the mutual care that took place in marriage. This relationship was more than casual acquaintance or association. This was a gathering of people that became a family. As people like Joshua and Sarah turned to Christ, they were often ostracized from their families and friends. Faced with life in isolation, they were welcomed into a new community. And the community met where families gather, a home.

For many of us the term *fellowship* draws us back to musty church basements with linoleum tile, cold metal chairs, and paper tablecloths. As a child I did not want to attend the church fellowships. The food was gross. The

25

convergence of smells from all the lukewarm casseroles still sends shivers down my spine. What Luke describes was not that! The community helped each member connect with one another.

As an outward sign of their fellowship, the new community shared meals together. These followers of Christ were devoted to "the breaking of bread." It's odd that Luke would include this detail. We often want to spiritualize it and suggest that he was referring to the Lord's Supper. However, it's more likely that he is describing the first potluck. The meal probably included communion, but that took place within a larger, shared meal.[1] In a time when food was not easy to come by, when people shared what they had, they were demonstrating trust that God would continue to provide.

Food has a kindling effect. It can turn a dull gathering full of people searching for an exit into a party where everyone is participating. Sharing a meal together demonstrates that this gathering was more than an information-gathering session. It was a further confirmation of the community that God was going to form. You may not have known of this biblical precedent for coffee and brownies in small groups!

The Spiritual Growth Pattern: Changing

It wasn't just community the first Christians were devoted to. They were also committed to growing in Christ. As the church began, the only written documents were Old Testament scrolls. The Gospels wouldn't be written for another twenty or thirty years. Paul was still a critic and persecutor of Christians, not the inspirational author of future New Testament letters. Much of what would become the New Testament existed in the oral teachings of the apostles. As they repeated the stories and teachings of Jesus, people like our fictional Joshua, Sarah, Ben, and Simeon "devoted" themselves to what was taught. The believers helped each other remember what was said at the temple. They asked each other for wise counsel.

As followers of Jesus they wanted to become more like him. They knew they needed to change, and the teaching would help them identify the places in their lives where they needed to grow. You can imagine how, as these Christ followers huddled in the temple courtyard, John and Peter repeated the Sermon on the Mount or the parables. They talked about gracious living and being the same sort of person on the inside as you are on the outside.

No doubt, when the believers gathered later in homes, they rehashed the apostles' teachings and began to make application to their everyday lives in these gatherings. Did Jesus really intend for us to forgive so many times that we would quit counting? What does it mean to live a meek life? Is it possible that God really celebrates when a person repents and turns to him? How do we demonstrate love to friends and family who have rejected us? How do we show love to people who treat us badly? The home gathering was intent on helping people change to become more like Christ.

The Missional Pattern: Cultivating

An extraordinary thing happened to the community of Christ followers. As a result of their devotion to Christ and one another, God increased their membership. Luke said that every day God added to their number. Undoubtedly, the Holy Spirit did a miraculous work drawing hundreds and thousands of people to God. However, the changed lives and the rich relational community became an attractive force in the city of Jerusalem. Word spread of the generosity of believers, of transformed lives, and of extreme care for one another. The community of believers reached out to their friends, family, and neighbors and told them about Jesus. They became missional.

The Next Fifteen Hundred Years

About forty years after Luke described this first phase of the church, the temple was destroyed and with it the venue for large gatherings of Christ followers. For nearly three more centuries the church was based in homes. Followers of Christ were considered enemies of Rome and persecuted harshly. Large public gatherings were not safe. Towns such as Jerusalem, Rome, or Ephesus might have had thousands of Christians, but each church would be made up of ten to thirty people who met in homes. It would be illegal for churches to own property until the first "Christian" emperor emerged centuries later. Contrary to what we might expect, Christianity flourished during this time of oppression. With no structures or large, formal worship services, the followers of Christ multiplied. Not by conquest or force but by the dramatic impact of Christ and his church in the lives of the believers. During the first few centuries Luke's words were both poetic and prophetic: "And the Lord added to their number daily those who were being saved" (Acts 2:47).

When Constantine legalized Christianity in 313, the church was never the same. As the state religion, Christianity was altered dramatically. The pattern of home fellowships diminished and was replaced with a system focused on public worship led by official clergy. Councils were formed and creeds were written. The books that make up the Bible were officially confirmed. Persecution ended and Christianity entered a favored status in Europe.

All of that is good, right? you might be wondering. *I mean, why wouldn't it be good for Christianity to be legal?* Well, of course, the freedom to believe without oppression was good, but some unfortunate developments emerged. For the next twelve hundred years the notion of the priesthood of believers was lost. The church became dependent on trained, ordained ministers who took over the function of helping people grow. Small, home-based community gave way to large gatherings. Circles of fellowship became forward-facing lines of observers. While the church at this time created beautiful liturgy and art and wrote profound doctrinal works, for the most part, community life was severely diminished. The New Testament picture of community life described by Luke, Paul, and Peter fell by the wayside.

A Renewed Hope

Fast-forward twelve hundred years after Christianity was legalized. With the Reformation in the 1500s, elements of community life began to reemerge. Martin Luther preached heavily on the priesthood of all believers. He taught that the true church was invisible and that it was within the masses that showed up for public worship. It was a dramatic shift from the notion that everyone in the empire was a Christian. He began to prepare the way for the sincere followers of Christ to find each other and reinforce each other's faith in settings outside of worship. While he never implemented small groups, he taught the value of gathering with the true faithful.[2]

By the 1700s John Wesley developed a thorough small group structure. As the former Anglican minister began to reach an audience that was outside of the church, he realized the weekly worship service was not enough to spiritually enrich the new believers. He used classes and groups to help people connect and change. His groups offered community but demanded high commitment and accountability. The intensity and complexity of his system also led to its demise.

In the late 1870s a new movement emerged at Cambridge University. A group of students began to pray, study the Bible together, and share their faith with others.[3] Within eighty years small group ministries were springing up at colleges and universities all over North America and the United Kingdom.

During the rise of these ministries, many churches were still using a classroom education style to help grow believers. In smaller churches many of these adult Sunday schools functioned like small groups do today. Participants shared life with one another and studied the Scriptures. However, many classes outgrew the ability to foster interpersonal relationships. There simply wasn't time for participants to talk about life and complete a lesson. The emphasis in most classroom settings was on increasing head knowledge and less on heart involvement.

Recent Past

Many statistics today confirm that those who attend church don't live much differently than those who do not participate in a church at all. A new model of development is needed. But perhaps more than a new model of spiritual formation, we need to restore an ancient one. Like the believers in Jerusalem two thousand years ago, we need to gather for teaching and retreat to homes so that we connect with other believers, change to become more like Christ, and cultivate a missional life.

It's extremely important to recognize that this brief history lesson covered community movements in what is often called the Western church. The church in Asia, Africa, and South America often resembles the community-oriented church of the first few centuries. In China in particular, the house church movement is measured in the millions of participants. In South Korea, home to the largest church in the world, small groups are an integral part of spiritual life. In Africa and South America small gatherings of Christ followers are a normal feature of the spiritual life. It seems the only places we need to create a small groups strategy is Europe and America, where community, in general, is depleted. Some have suggested that in the West, technology, the fast pace of life, and focus on consuming material goods has squelched community. Certainly, Asia, Africa, and the rest of the developing world have issues, but a deep need for a community strategy isn't one of them.

Back Then and Up Ahead

What can we learn from our history? First, small gatherings of believers, meeting in each other's homes, were part of the earliest fabric of the church. During the first three hundred years, home-based fellowships were the norm, not the exception. Without the church meeting in homes there was no church.

The second lesson has to do with the invisible church, as Luther called it. People who seek to grow in their faith need a community that merges both the truth of Scripture and the ability to discuss the challenges of life. Believers need a special place to encourage one another to stay on the spiritual path. The writer of Hebrews addresses this when he says, "Let us consider how we may spur one another on toward love and good deeds" (Heb. 10:24). These communities have located the Scriptures as their central curriculum. The early church passed on the oral Scriptures as they repeated the stories told by the apostles. Later, they passed around the letters written by Paul, Peter, John, and James. In fact, one of the factors that helped decide if a letter should be part of the New Testament was how widely read and accepted it was by these churches. The Scriptures became central to the Protestant Reformation, and all the groups that emerged after Luther continued a focus on the Bible. This is still true for strong groups.

Finally, healthy groups help each member live a missional life. The strongest communities throughout the history of the church weren't focused just on their own needs and interests but also maintained an outward focus. From the first church in Jerusalem in the 30s AD to gatherings of college students at Cambridge nearly nineteen hundred years later, faithful followers of Christ needed a space to refresh and recharge as they engaged a culture for Christ. If the apostle Paul was discouraged when trying to live the missional life on his own (see 2 Tim. 4:9–21), how much more will we be without a Christian community?

Real Simple

As we look back at history, we might wonder what's so simple about groups? In fact, small gatherings of believers look difficult, complicated, and most of the time absent from the church. Why should we bother? What's simple about it? I've wondered the same questions. But I come back to the same answers.

It's biblical. From the time of Moses to the time of Paul, groups in various forms and by different names have been used by God to grow his people.

It's effective. Small gatherings of believers have been around for thousands of years—particularly when the church was thriving. Lives change. Missionary movements emerge.

We need it. In a world full of technology that helps us communicate in nearly limitless ways, we seem more disjointed and isolated than ever. As we move into a new era filled with new questions, the watching world is tired of talk and evidence and sermons and debate. Yet it is still aching for what only Christ can bring. Perhaps the most effective way for us to make the love of Jesus real in these times is by manifesting that love in simple, missional small groups.

part 1

connecting

The Relational Pattern

con * nect [kuh-nekt]

The process of developing relationships with
an identified group of people.

2

the pattern of connecting

Overcoming Obstacles, Imagining Possibilities

There is a gnawing ache within each of us to connect in a meaningful way with someone else. This need is most noticeable when it is not met. We often try to cover the need for community with something else. We live vicariously through television or film. We try to occupy ourselves with work or shopping or food or alcohol. But it is always there: a deep, burning need to know and be known.

However, the whole notion of entering a growing relationship with a group of people in which I will show love, grace, and submission is countercultural. Instead, our culture prides itself on independence—not community. Every July 4 we celebrate as a nation telling another nation, "We don't need you!" This independence seeps into all areas of our lives, from popular images of cowboys and action heroes to classic songs like "Desperado." We are a people in denial. We demand our rights, even if our rights infringe on the rights of others. We seek self-fulfillment over community fulfillment.

Biblical values such as community and submission stand in stark contrast to some of our cultural values. Star athletes choose teams based upon who will pay the most, not where they can make the biggest contribution. Most reality shows are based on how much you can deceive and connive, not serve and share. And all the while we ache. We long for the thing right in front of us.

Perhaps if we naturally developed healthy community, the need for small groups would diminish. If our tendency was to seek out other followers of Christ on whom we would mutually depend and challenge, we wouldn't need groups. Even when we do seek community, we often don't seek healthy ones that will encourage us.

It shouldn't surprise us that connecting in a group is hard. Because we bear the image of God, we need community, and because we live in a world plagued by sin, the very thing we need is hard to get. We simultaneously want growing relationships and we want our way. Ralph Waldo Emerson wrote, "Every man alone is sincere. At the entrance of a second hypocrisy begins."[1] Connecting with others is often wrought with peril.

Peter: A Small Group Leader

Dave sat in the mop closet of his residence hall sobbing. He had never felt so alone. Sure, plenty of people knew him. He was an athlete and a student leader at a small Christian liberal arts school. He was a great student and always seemed to have a girlfriend. "But I was alone," Dave later recounted to me. That night there was an open house in his dorm, but no one stopped by to visit him. His friends stopped by another room and never migrated to his. It hit him later that evening that he knew plenty of people but lacked community.[2] Most of his relationships were based on the convenience of class schedule and his popularity.

"The funny thing was," Dave recalled, "I had Jesus; wasn't that enough?" Here's the thing. Jesus points people to community; he started one himself (the twelve disciples and others), and he is constantly pointing his followers to other people.

Take Peter, for example. After the resurrection Jesus appeared to Peter on the shore of the Sea of Galilee (John 21:15–18). He asked Peter a simple question: "Do you love me?" Peter said he did. What's interesting is that Jesus was not satisfied with Peter's reply. It wasn't enough for Peter to have a relationship with Jesus—he needed to relate to Jesus' followers. Peter needed to demonstrate his love for Christ by caring for the followers of Christ. "Then feed my sheep," Jesus replied.

This passage has specific implications for small group leaders. Jesus challenged Peter to invest in a group of people—to shepherd a flock. Good shepherding requires careful observation and ongoing care. Peter had to demonstrate his love for Jesus in his love for the sheep God put in front of him. I doubt Jesus was telling Peter to randomly care for people he stumbled across. If a shepherd is called to feed and care for a flock, it is a flock he knows. He is aware of their needs. This takes proximity. It takes connection. The primary way for Peter to show that he loved Jesus was to care for people he knew.

It would be easy to dismiss this as a unique command for Peter. Or to assume it was Jesus' way of restoring Peter after he denied he knew Jesus three times. But the story contains a challenge for each of us. If we say we love God, we should look for ways to care for others. Like Peter, we can offer mere words that affirm our love of God (and our love of people), but if the people don't have names, do we really love them? If we don't love a flock of people, how can we show our love of God?

If anyone captured the relationship between love of God and love of people, the apostle John did.

If someone says, "I love God," but hates a Christian brother or sister, that person is a liar; for if we don't love people we can see, how can we love God, whom we cannot see? And he has given us this command: Those who love God must also love their Christian brothers and sisters.

1 John 4:20–21 NLT

We have to be honest. There are times when it would be easier if we could love God and ignore our spiritual family. They can be irritating and exhausting. They let us down. Sometimes they gossip about us. They require that we adjust our lives for them. Sometimes connecting in a community of believers feels like it's more trouble than it's worth. But Jesus whispers in the background, "If you love me, you'll love them."

What Kills Our Connection?

Time

If connecting with a community of people is so important, why is it so hard? Shouldn't it be easy to help people connect in our groups if people are created for community?

I remember standing in the atrium of our church, attempting to involve a young couple in a group. I wouldn't have harassed the guy if he hadn't walked directly up to me and begun conversing about groups. They were a young couple in need of some good relationships, and they were deeply interested in the new study we were offering.

"Here's a sign-up card. All you have to do is fill this out, show up Sunday night, and we'll connect with some other great people," I said as I attempted to pass a card toward him.

His face scrunched up in sort of a disappointed response. "Will you be offering this study again?" he asked.

"I'm afraid not. Sure, if you join a group they can pick it up later, but it's not as likely. They'll probably grab whatever study we're offering at that time. If you're interested, why don't you try it out?" I nearly begged him.

"It's just that we're so busy right now." He shrugged as he walked away.

I was left wondering what will make later less busy. Let's face it, life is busy! When we are trying to help people connect to our groups, there are plenty of other things that compete for their time. From extra hours at work and long commutes to kids' sports and special events, there is no shortage of things to spend time on. I even know people who won't join a group because it meets on the night of their favorite TV show![3]

The number one explanation for missing a group is that something else came up. Sometimes it's legitimate and sometimes it's just an excuse. We never know. One leader told me that on a number of occasions Kevin called half an hour before the group meeting to tell the leader he wouldn't be able to make it because his parents had stopped by unexpectedly. That would have been understandable if Kevin's folks had lived hours away—but they lived fifteen minutes away! It wasn't a special thing to have them stop by, but it provided an excuse for Kevin to skip.

Relational Exhaustion

Nearly all of us already have family and friends besides our group. Our relationship plate can get very full very fast. It has made me wonder: if we are relationally tapped, why is a group helpful?

Groups have something to offer even those who have good friends and close family. Meet "Teresa." By all accounts Teresa came from a great family. She went to college and then returned to her hometown to begin a promising career as an accountant. She often spent an evening or two with her family enjoying a meal or playing a game. Most weekends she hung out with friends at coffee shops or attending civic theater events together. By government statistics, Teresa was an oddity. She had a good family and plenty of friends.

However, to co-workers Teresa was a pain. Her sarcastic attitude and jabbing sense of humor were a wet blanket on meetings. If she was eating lunch in the break room, co-workers were likely to grab their lunch from the refrigerator and eat at their desks. Teresa's co-workers knew a little-known secret: often friends and family are not likely to help us become better people.

Our family knows us well. They know our dark side. They know our failures. Teresa's family knew she was sarcastic. They knew she had a biting sense of humor. But they had grown used to it. As it had developed over the years, they learned to tune it out. They had come to anticipate her comments. It's not that her mother really liked that side of Teresa, but she had grown numb to it. In fact, she often didn't even notice her daughter's occasional tirades.

Her brother Allen noticed. And he wasn't numb to it. It bothered him, but he was afraid to say anything to her for fear that it would ruin the upcoming Thanksgiving holiday. Several years earlier he had pulled her aside and challenged the way she interacted with others. It did not go well. Teresa listed all of Allen's faults and wouldn't talk to him for over a month. Allen was certain if he addressed Teresa's problem—if he challenged her to become more like Christ—she would attack him again and likely cause upset among the whole family.

Teresa's friends weren't much better. The only difference is that they didn't really notice her sarcasm. Probably because they shared it. They had all honed the art of verbal jabs. The banter at the coffee shop they frequented was full of affectionate put-downs. That sounds odd to most of us, but to them it was part of who they were. People seated nearby at Starbucks thought they were a pretty disparaging bunch, but Teresa and her friends thought they were good friends enjoying a latte.

We are all like Teresa. Few of us live in families that are strong enough or open enough to be truly honest. It doesn't mean that our families are utter failures. It simply means most families are not good at helping adult family members attain their greatest potential in their walk with Christ. Since family is stuck with us, they often don't want to ruin the next thirty years in a family feud.

And just like Teresa we tend to choose friends who are like us. In high school I had a foul mouth. I'm not talking PG-13 mouth. I'm talking R-rated, every-other-word foul mouth. I don't recall any of my friends pulling me aside and challenging my vocabulary. Probably because they had R-rated mouths too. It's not that friends aren't willing to challenge us, and it's not that they don't want to see us grow; it's just that often they share the same blind spots and growth areas.

A small group occupies a unique relational space. If the members connect enough in the group to really know each other—and if they are willing to take a risk—they can help each other grow. They can enjoy a connecting community and help us see our blind spots. If Teresa joins a group she might find people who begin to know her, warts and all. And while loving her, they might take the risk and help her change. That begins to hint at the second pattern—change—which I will talk about in the next part.

Weirdos

If you've read small groups books, you know "weirdos" are called all sorts of things: EGR, or "Extra Grace Required" people, ECR, or "Extra Care Required" people, the "as is" people, project people, the needy people, and occasionally the EBH—the "Emotional Black Hole." Whatever the term, we know what it really means: weird. We don't want to give these people our email address or cell phone number, much less invite them into our group. Nothing can kill a group before it connects like a weird person or two.

Larry came to be nicknamed "End Times Larry." It was suggested that he gave himself the nickname to underscore his favorite hobby—you guessed it, the end times. He was the only person saddened that they quit writing *Left Behind* books. He was certain on New Year's Eve of 1999 that the end was minutes away. For the next two years he ate the stockpile of rice and bottled water. It didn't matter what topic the group was discussing, you could always count on Larry to bring it around to the fact that we were living in "the last days." Whether it was the Detroit Lions finally winning a football game or a great sale on jeans at the Gap, or a Scripture passage in Ephesians—it all had to do with Jesus coming back again. And perhaps he was right; after all, the return of Christ is a pretty consistent theme in the New Testament. But it had become so cliché for him that the group quit listening to what he was saying. He was weird.

Some of us have an End Times Larry in our group. Or perhaps it's emotionally needy Ned who "just wants a special woman to share his life with." Or chatty Cathy who loves to talk. Or Bob the Bible expert. Or Bill the amateur comedian (that's me). We sometimes avoid community out of fear that we'll end up in a group full of people like that.

Bill Donahue, author and speaker, has often said that if you can't identify the "extra grace required" person in your groups it's because it's *you.* Maybe John Ortberg said it best in his book *Everybody's Normal Till You Get to Know Them.* John says we all have an "as-is" tag. Like the seconds rack at the back of a department store, we are all slightly imperfect. We are all weird.

We may not have a pathological weirdo—the person who is clinically weird in such a way that they will sap all the energy from a group and set up a tent in your backyard. Groups are filled with normally weird people. But I have to be honest: odd people do join small groups. And sometimes they end up in our group. But sometimes those are the very people we need in our lives to help us grow closer to Christ.

Tim and Connie Smith seemed like fairly normal people on the surface. Tim was a tool and die maker and Connie was a stay at home mom who dedicated herself to homeschooling the kids. At first they were just different, but soon the group realized that the Smiths were weird. It started with little personality quirks but evolved as the group got to know them. What the group discovered over time was that the Smiths' home was a disaster, they had a poor work ethic, and financially they were inches from ruin. Most groups would be overwhelmed by this level of weird.

When I sat down to talk with Jerry and Sheryl, the leaders of the small group, they began to reveal the challenges of having the Smiths in the group. They obviously stood out in the group. The rest of the group was primarily professional people. It wasn't just a matter of income and career—the Smiths had different values and were relationally immature, which showed in the way they interacted in the group. It was not simply a matter of helping mow an overgrown lawn— there were deep issues at play.

I braced myself, expecting Jerry to tell me he wanted me to remove the Smiths from his group. *Where will I put them if this group rejects them?* I wondered. Then Jerry shocked me. He explained that the rest of his group had prayerfully considered how they could best help the family. A couple of the more mechanical people were going to help with the house, a person with some financial skills was going to offer to guide and coach them in that area, and an expert in early childhood development was going to offer her support with the education of the children. The group decided that God wanted to teach them about the love of Jesus through placing these strange people in their group.

As with Jesus' challenge to Peter in John 21, Jerry and Sheryl's group accepted the opportunity to show love for Jesus by taking care of some of his sheep. I wish the story had a great ending. Ultimately Tim and Connie were offended that the group wanted to help them. It insinuated that they had a problem (which was obvious to all). Eventually the Smiths exited that group. But it was a defining moment that helped Jerry and Sheryl's group grow in their connection with each other.

What Does It Look Like to Connect?

The pattern of connecting is essential if we want to show that we love God and live consistently with how he wired us. It is the relational pattern of a healthy small group. Connecting is simply a growing relationship with an identified group of people who meet regularly. It's not complicated at all. As we help our group connect, we help build relational bridges between the people in our group.

Is It All about Intimacy?

I was very reluctant to invite Doug to our new group. The four of us who were already in a small group were fairly average, middle-class guys. Doug was a handsome guy with great teeth! And he was wealthy. He owned a construction company that seemed to be doing well. He lived on a large estate, drove new vehicles, and went on great vacations. But Josh insisted we invite him. I was certain that I was wasting Doug's time (and my own). Why would he want to hang out with us?

After a month of harassment from Josh, I finally called him. I was relieved to catch Doug's voice mail. My message was something like, "Hey Doug, it's Bill Search, and you probably aren't interested and probably too busy so if you decline, I understand, but if you want to, we'd like to invite you to our guys group." What I wanted to say was, "Hey, Doug, you're probably too rich and cool for this, but if you want to lower yourself to join a few losers on Wednesday mornings, we'd be honored to have you."

I was shocked when he called back. And I was even more shocked when he accepted our invitation. What I didn't anticipate was how God was drawing us together. As a group we met every week, spent part of the time reading the Scripture together, and then discussed it. Doug was like a thirsty man in the desert. He wasn't satisfied with reading and commenting. Would we live it out? Rather quickly we caught his passion. It started as a weekly meeting, but quickly we found ourselves committed to the group. I don't remember when it happened, but we began to belong to each other. The meeting would stretch past the allotted time. We'd call each other during the week. We became brothers. And we knew it was a sacred thing that not everyone who enters a group can say.

Within a couple of years each one of us was facing a personal struggle. Work. Business. Finances. Doubts. Calling. And with each issue we encouraged and challenged each other to pursue Christ. The honesty flowed out of a deep level of connecting.

This should not come as a surprise. Throughout the Scriptures God brought key relationships together to help his servants manage through challenging situations. When God called Moses from Sinai to return to Egypt and lead his people out of Egypt, he also sent Aaron to be a partner in ministry. While David was a king in waiting—anointed but not ruling—he was surrounded by a devoted group of mighty men. When Mary was told she was pregnant with the Messiah, God led her to her cousin Elizabeth's, where they could encourage and support each other. Paul traveled with an entourage and while imprisoned begged an old friend to loan him a former slave as a friend and partner in ministry. But it's not just Bible celebrities who God leads into community to face life's challenges.

And life *is* full of challenges. Careers that pay the bills but don't fulfill. Marriages that produce children but an unhappy intimate life. Children with lots of toys but a complaining attitude. Families that get together but don't love each other.

Friends who listen to problems but don't keep secrets. But challenges are best not faced alone.

I learned something else in that group. Some groups connect like a family. A deep bond develops. Group members share hidden pain. Personal struggles. Anxieties no one else is aware of. These groups find it natural to confess sin and confront and challenge each other. They are intimate, honest, and give a strong sense of belonging.

And yet, if the standard for connecting is deep, vulnerable confession, few groups would qualify as connecting. After all, the first couples group I was part of was a good community and helpful to my spiritual growth, but I wouldn't really call it "intimate." The group with Josh and Doug was my first group that I would describe as intimate. I've been part of nearly a dozen groups, but none has replicated this experience. That's okay! Those other groups taught me other things. They weren't failures. Instead of determining the strength of a group on descriptors like "intimacy, openness, and vulnerability," can we honestly acknowledge that connecting isn't a small bull's-eye but a relational pattern that has varying degrees of intensity? It's not a tiny target; it's a broad goal.

The Bull's-Eye

For many years the terms "small group" and "intimacy" were used in the same breath. Sure, some groups became deeply intimate, but for many more groups, the members were more like casual friends. If your group doesn't feel like a family of brothers and sisters, your group is not a failure. It's good if you hope for a group of open, honest people who freely share life's struggles with each other. But you should also celebrate if you have a group of people that just keeps showing up! We can enjoy the broad range of a connecting group.

When most groups begin, they feel awkward and forced. We wonder if we'll ever feel comfortable with these new relationships. We gather with strangers in a living room and then ask them to share their opinions and feelings. That's pretty weird when you think about it. Then we open up the Bible, read it together, and then discuss how we can apply it to our lives. All the while we're hoping that the other people in the group don't think we're dumb or ignorant. It sure doesn't feel like the New Testament community Luke described in Acts 2, does it? But that's how most groups start. In the first handful of months, most groups feel like a meeting or a class. As a leader you sense they are holding back and not sharing their true thoughts. And this is the only community some will know. While others want more, for some groups just having people show up week after week is something to be happy about. I think it's important to avoid the impulse to belittle or shame the group that feels more like a meeting than a community. Let's pause here and be happy when people keep showing up for our group, participating in the discussion, and sharing a little bit of life with one another—that's a good thing!

Some groups move past regular attendance and participation and form a tighter relational bond with each other. They love to connect outside of the group and talk on the phone often. Sure, the group meeting is important, but it's really an excuse to get together. The members know more than just simple facts about each other (like kids' names and occupations), and they talk about hobbies, interests, and passions. Conversation is natural and not forced. If anything, the questions in the Bible discussion guide sometimes get in the way of the personal application the group gravitates toward.

Still other groups feel like family. They share more than stories—they've been known to help each other in very practical ways. Perhaps they help with home upkeep or remodeling, or share with each other if a person has a financial need. Family-like groups sometimes vacation together, eat together, and take any excuse just to be together.

The point here is, the bull's-eye is huge! We don't prize only groups that feel like families. We live in a relationally fractured world, so just having a group of people where we know names and meet together regularly is a positive thing. For some, connecting is a frequent gathering for a study and for others it's a family of people who are constantly in each other's lives. As I will explain in the other sections, some groups are focused on another pattern and can only spend a certain amount of energy on the pattern of connecting. The point isn't to achieve depth in all three patterns but simply to engage each pattern. I'll say more on this later.

Dangerous Expectations

When we talk about connecting, we have to embrace the tension that some groups will become close relationally and others will not. A good group might be made up of people who simply show up. If I could change one thing about small groups as they are currently practiced, it would be the expectation that the members will become close friends. It's great if this happens, and it's fine if it doesn't.

After graduate school I moved to Calvin College in Grand Rapids, Michigan, to work as a resident director. The job involved advising students who were struggling with relational issues. One evening a young woman stopped by my office, very upset. She needed a new roommate. After I asked her to explain why, she shared a laundry list of issues. Her roommate was a slob, used her computer without asking, and talked on the phone when she was trying to study. Pretty common issues for roommates. As I talked with her more, I got to the heart of the issue. This sweet young girl came to the college her mother attended, the same college where her mother forged what became a lifelong friendship with her first roommate. This girl grew up thinking of Mom's roommate as an aunt. The real issue wasn't a dirty room or annoying phone calls. She came to college hoping for a deep, intimate friendship and quickly realized that was unlikely to occur with her assigned roommate. Unmet relational expectations are not just a problem for college freshmen; they're a problem for many small groups.

Look, somehow we got this idea that a group is not successful unless it becomes really intimate and familial. Let me give you permission to lead a group that is neither of those things. If your group becomes that, great, but some groups will never become that. They will be good, safe places for people to discuss important things and have some fun, but they will never be family-like. Others will focus on serving the community around them. That's fine too. There are a whole host of ways for people to connect; we don't have to share the deepest, darkest parts of ourselves to truly connect.

Creating a Safe Relational Space

So how can we help our participants connect on a level that works for our group? Whether our group feels like they are lightly attached to each other or whether they have become like a close-knit family, what can we do as group leaders to help build the relational connection? The next chapter is dedicated to the practical things we can do to help people connect, but what are the more general ways that connecting takes place in a group?

Create a Comfortable Place

We can use big words like *authentic, confidential, honest,* and *safe,* but ultimately what we mean is that we hope people feel comfortable in our group! If our members aren't comfortable—physically and emotionally—then they probably won't connect. Most of us won't go back to a group if it makes us uptight or nervous. As we lead, we should address the physical concerns first. It's pretty easy to make sure we

49

have adequate lighting and a place for everyone to sit. But we should also help make our group a comfortable place emotionally.

One of my old small group leaders, Mike, was a natural at helping group members feel comfortable. "It bothers me," I remember him saying to our group one evening, "that I sometimes make decisions based on how my wife will respond." I'll always remember that transparency. As we talked about what motivated us to do the right thing, he modeled for the group that we didn't have to have it all figured out—we didn't have to give the answer that everyone expected. In fact, after he was so honest, it would have been impossible to drop in a cliché like, "Well, whatever the Bible says to do, that's what I try to do." While that kind of reply might be theologically correct, it is rarely honest.

At other times I recall Mike responding to other members' answers by asking "Is that what you really think?" when he sensed that we were just giving a good "church" answer that didn't reflect our true feelings. He didn't ask with a mean spirit. Maybe it was his schoolteacher training and his "Mr. Clean" look-alike appearance, but he could furrow his brow, give a wry smile, and get to the truth. Mike gently encouraged us to drop our guards and share with the group who we really were and what we really thought. Our own personal walls keep us from connecting, and I think Mike knew that the key to building the relational pattern started with how he led the group. As leaders, like Mike, we can model the level of honesty we hope to hear, and we can encourage our members to share their real thoughts. If we do this graciously, we can help remove the pretense that haunts some groups and allow our members to drop their guards. Of course, small group covenants or agreements are great tools to help us set that pattern at the start, but ongoing modeling and questions help keep a group emotionally comfortable. When we are comfortable in our group, we invite our fellow members to relax.

Share Snapshots

Whenever I visit a friend's home, I look for the photo albums. I love to look at wedding photos from ten years ago. Even better is when you stumble upon your friend's prom pictures—big hair and poofy sleeves—ah, the fun of humiliating pictures! A couple of years before my grandfather passed away, I sat down with him and pawed through old photos. I would hand him a picture and ask, "Who's this?" And a story would emerge. The photo would be a springboard into five other stories. I would hand him another photo of a car (my grandfather loved cars), and he would describe how much he paid for it, the extra features he added to it, and when he traded it in. I learned more about my grandpa from that small shoe box than the seventeen years of stories before that.

When we lead our groups, we help people connect when we give them the space to share their snapshots with the group. No, I don't mean literal photos (though that's fine too). When we reveal small details about ourselves, we are sharing "snapshots."[4] It's as if we pull out our personal photo album and hold up a picture of ourselves, inviting others to compare their photos. When we tell others in our group what we collect, or what we listen to on the radio, or where we would like to retire, or what sports team should win the Super Bowl, we are lifting up snapshots. Then they pull out their collection of photos and hold them up. In the process we realize that perhaps we share a similar hobby, or musical tastes, or skills. The point is, we begin to connect with people as we find our common interests and experiences. These shared photos link our stories together and help our members form a community with one another.

As you lead a small group, your role is not to force connection but to facilitate a safe relational space. You can't make your group belong to one another, but you can create a space where people feel comfortable enough that they want to return. The next chapter focuses on the practical things you can do to help your group connect with each other.

3

the nuts and bolts of connecting

Helping People Form Relational Bonds

The Connecting Continuum

I experienced an intimate community for the first time when I formed a group with my friends Josh and Doug. I shared thoughts hidden from nearly everyone (but my wife) and confessed sins that I didn't plan to talk about with any human. I also had a great small group experience with several couples who met together nearly twice a month for over two years. We didn't necessarily talk about our deepest secrets, but we still had a great time together. One group experience isn't necessarily better than another. We are all different people, and therefore we are going to have different group expectations and experiences. We should think of connecting as a continuum with varying degrees of intensity. More intense isn't better or worse than less intense experiences. Our goal as leaders should be to include the connecting pattern at the degree of intensity right for our group.

When a group first forms, building the connection pattern is imperative. No matter how great our vision for our group, if people don't relationally connect with each other, they will exit the group. Our goal as group leaders should be to help groups form the connecting pattern as quickly as they can. While some groups will end, most will continue if we do a few simple things to help our participants connect. Before we explore some of those simple things, let's take a closer look at the phases of connecting the typical group goes through.

Meet

Attending a small group for the first time is one of the scariest experiences you'll live through. Sure, you like your group now, but do you remember that first meeting? I was scared out of my skull. I remember the whole drive to the hosts' home, hoping the directions would be wrong or that I would get lost. I doubt my anxiety is unique.

The first phase of the connect pattern is to *meet* with one another. During this phase, group members treat the group just like that: a meeting. It's an event they attend, not a community they are emotionally attached to. Sure, they gather often, discuss the Bible, and get to know each other, but if the leader doesn't schedule the next meeting, the group is over. It's the meeting that holds the group together. The relational bonds are very vulnerable during this phase, and it's easy to get out.

I would like you to meet one group as they travel through these phases together. Jennifer and Eric were frustrated with their group. After three months of meeting together, the group was far from relational bliss. Yeah, everyone showed up each week, and while they were there the members would participate in the discussion. But as soon as the session ended, everyone headed for the door. Eric and Jennifer dreamed of community and what they got was a weekly event. They recognized, however, that most groups start out as nothing more than a regular gathering. All of us are relationally cautious when we first come to a small group; that's natural. Some people will *always* treat the group as a meeting and won't emotionally invest. Hopefully our groups are diverse enough to accept them too.

Commit

As a group connects, over time the members may begin to *commit* to one another. Sometimes it takes months and sometimes it takes minutes, but the people in a group moving along the connecting pattern begin to form closer relational ties. In the committing phase we begin to show interest in each other's stories and connect both inside and outside of the group meeting. The group does not hinge upon the meeting, and if the group takes a break at Christmas, the members are still committed to one another. They may not have a family-like connection, but friendship is beginning to form.

Let's return to Eric and Jennifer's group. After a few months they began to notice a surprising change. When their group ended at 8:00 p.m., people wouldn't bolt for the door; they'd stick around. In fact, it seemed like the party had just gotten started. Eric would brew a second pot of coffee (decaf this time) and the group members would settle in for more conversation. The group of twelve would become three mini groups of vibrant interaction. Four people stayed in the living room to debate politics, while five others escaped into the family room to turn on the remainder of the basketball game and talk sports. Two others went with Jennifer into the kitchen to check out her new stand mixer. Of course, all of this happened in the group meeting, but outside the meeting was where the fun was just beginning. Between email and the phone, members were connecting constantly. It was obvious to Eric and Jennifer that the relational bonds were beginning to strengthen within their group. They were enjoying the committing phase.

Belong

Some groups—though not all—enter another phase of connecting. When group members feel like they belong to one another, the relationship moves from friendship to a family-like attachment. When group members belong to one another, they feel like they are spiritual siblings. They demonstrate a concern for each other that rivals that of close families.

When Jennifer and Eric's group entered the belonging phase, it completely took them by surprise. Eric and Jennifer were thrilled just to lead a group that liked being together, but a deeper relational bond was demonstrated by the way the group rallied around Andrew and Bonnie. When Andrew broke his leg after falling off a ladder, it threw his family into a crisis. Andrew was a builder, and the broken leg meant he would be off work for more than a month. Sure, insurance helped, but it didn't help Bonnie manage the house and wrangle their three young sons. Without some help they were headed for a train wreck. That's when Jennifer and Eric realized their group was becoming a family. Three guys immediately volunteered to take care of all the landscaping. It was springtime, and for five weeks they took turns mowing the lawn, trimming the shrubs, and laying down mulch. Bonnie remarked that perhaps Andrew should have broken his leg earlier since the lawn had never looked so nice! The women in the group coordinated meals so that Bonnie could focus on one less thing. For more than a month Bonnie cooked little more than oatmeal in the morning. It seemed that the whole group crystallized around Bonnie and Andrew. No one served out of obligation; they relished the opportunity to lavish love upon the family. As Andrew healed, the group kept their close connection and continued to look for ways to serve one another.

Where Is Your Group?

Before you employ the nuts and bolts of connecting, it's helpful to explore your group's current phase of connecting.

- Are people coming to the group?
- Do they show up regularly?
- Do they participate in the discussion?

If you answered no to any of these, it's likely the group is in the meet phase.

- Do they hang around after group time?
- Are they sharing personal thoughts and opinions in the discussion?
- Are they showing an interest in each other?
- Do they know about each other's families?
- Do they communicate outside of the group meeting?

If you answered no to any of these, your group is likely in the commit phase.

- Do they spend time together outside of the group?
- Has your group gone on a retreat or some other day trip together?
- Do you know each other's life stories?
- Do people confess their struggles or sins in the group?

If you answered mostly yes to these, your group is likely in the belong phase.

What Can Help a Group Connect during the Meet Phase?

Conduct a Good Meeting

Good meetings involve everyone in the discussion. The point isn't to come up with just the right answer. It's to get people sharing what they really think—not to get them to share what they think we want to hear. One Sunday morning, the teacher asked her class of third graders, "What's brown, stores nuts for the winter, and scurries up trees?" Maggie lifted her hand and bashfully answered, "It sounds like a squirrel, but I'm going to guess, 'Jesus'?" We've all been in meetings like that. We sense that the leader doesn't want to hear our opinions or host an enthralling discussion. She's fishing for just the right answer.

My friend Garry Poole,[1] founder of the Seeker small groups movement, is an expert at leading discussion. Even though he knows more about leading small groups than most people will ever know, when he's seated at a table he's the one who talks the least. He has a brilliant theological mind, but his style is to get others talking about what interests them. To Garry it boils down to asking good questions and then listening. Mostly it's about listening. If people in the group believe that it's safe to share their thoughts, the discussion will be lively and engaging. Don't be afraid of silence, since most groups will take a while to trust that you really want to hear their thoughts. Since that so rarely happens, it will take a while to get that started.

Give Everyone a Job

In his book on job transitions, author Michael Watkins suggests that leaders employ "entanglement strategies" to involve members of their team. Don't dream of big leaps but of small steps. Each step creates what he calls a new "psychological reference point" for the next step.[2] In other words, when people contribute to the group, each time they develop a sense of ownership. All we need to do is ask Debbie to bring brownies. Ask Jim to find cheap notebooks to hold prayer requests. Ask Sherry to keep the group updated via email. Ask Chris to come up with a backyard game the group can play for half an hour at the next meeting. Ask Linda to pick up gourmet coffee. Ask Phil to lead the discussion next time. These small steps of involvement can move people closer to one another and a deeper sense that the group is theirs.

It's not about giving people insignificant busy work. As the members invest energy and time in the group, they will feel more of a bond and connection. They will sense that they are needed. And they are needed. As leaders, we often don't want to inconvenience others, and accidentally we keep them from investing their time and energy in the group. Over time, share the job of facilitating the discussion or of hosting the meeting. As others open their homes, they will reveal more of who they are. As they lead discussion, their personalities will emerge. These things will move toward more connection.

Pray for Each Other

Most people will be more open (or reveal how closed they are) when they are sharing prayer requests than at any other time. The key to making this time the most effective is providing good guidance. Early in the formation of the group, ask that prayer requests be personal. It's okay to pray for your great aunt if you love her and spend time with her. It's not okay if you make up prayer requests when you don't really care. No prayer for pets unless they eat at your dinner table and go on vacation with you. No prayers for a guy at work whose aunt's neighbor . . . you get the point. Lay out the guidelines early and you will have no problems.

I suggest that you set aside at least twenty minutes for the group to share prayer requests. It might be a good idea to pray as a large group only if one person is offering a short prayer. If you want more people to pray, it's often more helpful to break into small groups of three or four. Many people are not comfortable praying in a large group of people. If it's a mixed group, separate men and women from time to time and have them pray together. Let me encourage you to follow up on prayer requests through phone calls and emails, and at the next meeting. This communicates genuine interest, which underscores the connecting pattern. Furthermore, people are much more likely to be sincere in their requests for God's help (which is truly what "prayer requests" are!) when they know their words aren't wasted. Also, it's a good idea to encourage the group to pray for each other outside of the group time.

What Can Help a Group Connect during the Commit Phase?

Hang Out in Casual Settings

Whether or not you chose to give it an official title, it's important to spend time together outside of group time. Grill out before the group, go to a movie together, try a new restaurant together, celebrate a birthday or holiday together, grab coffee together. Whatever the reason or for no reason at all, spend additional time together. Rob and Amy lived a couple miles from Karyn and me. We met in our couples group and quickly formed a friendship. On the weekends we would rent movies and share meals. Within a couple of years we each welcomed our first baby into the family. We started hanging out more because our friends without kids didn't really want to hang out with a couple and a crying baby. Those casual interactions created a deeper bond than I would have expected.

Our experience was not unique. Building a quality connection often requires a quantity of time. Do you remember those arguments decades ago about whether it was more important for a parent to have quality or quantity time with their kids? Finally some wise person pointed out the obvious that you can't guarantee quality time, it occurs within the quantity time. We probably won't create quality relationships in a group that meets a couple of times a month for a few hours. Hanging out together outside of the normal group time gives us more opportunity to build better relational ties.

Sub-Group during the Meeting Time

The larger a group gets, the less people can participate. If a group has twelve members and meets for two hours, each person gets only ten minutes to talk. Since some people are quieter, they won't talk more than two minutes. And other people, like me, will steal their other eight minutes. If you split the group, you can double the time each person has. Even if you only split the group for half of the meeting time, you're still increasing the sharing opportunity by 50 percent!

"My group's just not connecting. I can't get anyone to talk," Steve groaned. Initially he was excited to lead. He was a sharp, growing Christian who warmly welcomed others. But his welcoming spirit was part of the problem. His group grew from six to twenty-three in a handful of months. Every Wednesday night the group would gather in his home for a couple of hours to watch a DVD of some great Bible teaching, and then Steve, to no avail, would attempt to lead a discussion. "It was easier when there were just six of us," Steve explained.

"So, why do you think it's harder to lead now?"

"Well, it's so big," Steve reasoned.

He was right. As the group got bigger, people didn't feel as comfortable sharing their opinions and ideas.

"What have you tried to help develop the connection?" I asked.

Steve described how he would often break the group into smaller groups to try to spur on conversation, but it seemed awkward. Since different people showed up each week, he rotated the smaller groups around so it was rare to be with the same smaller group two or three weeks in a row. Also, because time was tight, as soon as everyone was there he would start the video so they didn't miss the teaching time.

"You know, Steve, it's pretty obvious why people aren't connecting." His eyebrows raised; I went on. "First, most people just aren't comfortable talking in a group that big. Sub-grouping is a great solution, but rotating who's in those groups each week sets back any relational trust that is beginning to form. And finally, the lesson may be important, but if you don't focus on relationship building, you'll probably lose your learners."

"Duh!" was all he said, embarrassed at how obvious it was. Steve's not alone; we can easily overlook how simple it is to break into smaller groups within our group. Whether you try it out during part of the discussion or during prayer request time, breaking into smaller groups of four to six greatly increases the opportunity to participate.

What Can Help a Group Move toward the Belong Phase?

Take a Retreat or a Vacation Together

Moving from the normal routines and distractions can help us dig deeper relationally. Each year Colin and Nicole lead their group of young couples on a fall camping trip. Their group would work together to find a location, plan the food, and share camping equipment. Group members would rearrange their schedules to participate. People hit a relational depth late in the evening huddled around a campfire that they just won't typically hit in a regular meeting. Some groups are more into "condo-camping" and take short trips or vacations together. Riding in a car together for hours has a similar effect as a late-night campfire. Conversations come up driving down the highway that normally wouldn't while seated in a living room with Bibles in your lap.

Share Life Stories

Some groups have found it helpful to set aside several weeks so they can get to know each other better. At each meeting they put one person on the "hot seat" and invite them to share key events in their life. Some groups encourage creativity and share photos and symbols that represent significant experiences. Sometimes it's interactive, and the group members can ask questions during the presentation, and other times all the questions come at the end. I'll admit, it sounds strange, but in my experience it's like a relational booster rocket that propels people to connect.

My friend Carol felt the idea of sharing her life story seemed a bit absurd and forced. The group decided that it was time they really got to know one another. For a number of meetings in a row, they each took turns sharing the defining moments in their lives. Some brought photos and other mementos to display these hinge-points. Some talked of broken hearts, unmet dreams, and abuse. Woven into some of those same stories were beautiful moments such as when Christ entered their lives or when they met their spouse. Each person was given forty-five minutes to be on the hot seat. One man in the group, Todd, drew his life out on a scroll and would unroll a segment at a time. There were lots of tears. Carol resisted the idea. But as she thought through what she would tell about herself, she realized there were stories very few had ever heard. She began to see a recurring pattern of God's involvement in her life. As her turn came one evening, with tears, she described how God had provided for her during life's ups and downs.

Sharing life stories can feel forced. Some might think it sounds like silly psychobabble, but unless we have a space that encourages us to unload who we are, we probably won't do it. We'll reveal bits and pieces, but not in a way that invites others into our world. It's a very vulnerable experience, which is why it can profoundly draw us into a sense of belonging. It's a good way for a group that is growing together to continue that trend.

Reflection

Before moving on to the next pattern, take a few moments and reflect on these questions.

1. Read Acts 2:42–47. Luke presents a compelling picture of the early church. How does that image impact your expectations for your small group?

2. Read 1 John 4:20–21. How does John challenge you to love the people in your groups more? Is it hard to love any of them? Why?

3. Have you defined connecting in a community as intimacy? If so, what do you think of the connecting continuum?

4. What are the barriers that might keep your group from connecting?

5. Of the three phases of connecting (meet, commit, belong), where is your group?

6. How can you challenge your group to take the next step in the connecting pattern? What will you try to get them there?

changing

The Growth Pattern

change [cheynj]

The process of becoming more like
Jesus Christ.

4

the pattern of changing

Exploring How People Conform to the Image of Christ

Have you noticed how difficult change is? Remember how easy it seemed when you were young? In high school you could change social groups over a weekend at youth camp. In college you could lose twenty pounds in one semester by running every day after class. Or gain twenty pounds in one month by eating pizza at 11:00 p.m. every night. You could change majors with a piece of paper, careers with two weeks' notice. You could even change your residence by loading up your hatchback with all your worldly possessions. You could pick up a new habit (good or bad) and change girlfriends after a bad date. But change isn't so easy anymore, is it? My friend Rick found that out the hard way.

"You're a mama's boy!"

Rick was shocked! He was the son of a truck driver from a working-class community in Ohio; no one had ever called him a mama's boy before. Rick looked more like a bricklayer than the schoolteacher he was. He liked hunting and sports. The thought that he was overly attached to his mother rocked him. But the words hung out there waiting for his response.

It began simple enough. Newly married, Rick and Debbie got along great. They were both fresh out of college and early in their careers. A year into their marriage, Debbie suggested that they join a small group at their church. Reluctantly, Rick agreed. As the months passed, Rick felt more comfortable with the group, and the couple began to open up.

They had one perennial issue: Debbie felt Rick was too dependent on his mother. Debbie agreed Rick's mom was not the cliché caricature of an intrusive mother-in-law. In fact, his mother rarely called or visited without an invitation. But Rick would call his mother every day. And once a week he would take her out to lunch. It bugged Debbie that Rick was giving his mother the attention that she felt she deserved.

The tension over the issue occasionally escalated into a full-blown argument. In one quarrel Debbie suggested they tell their small group and let them give some advice. Rick was certain that the group would identify him as a good son grateful to a self-sacrificing mother, and identify his wife as a petty woman, jealous of a close parent-child bond. He was wrong.

One evening at their small group, Rick and Debbie shared their struggle. The other young couples listened patiently until Pete, a call-it-like-you-see-it construction foreman, blurted out, "You're a mama's boy!"

It took a few moments for Rick, a bit flushed with embarrassment, to realize that Pete was right. He was still hanging on to the apron strings, much to his dismay. The group encouraged and challenged him through the journey of truly leaving his father and mother and uniting with his wife. Over the next few months they would ask him, "So how often did you talk to your mom this week?" And as the weeks spread into months Rick successfully bonded more with his wife.

Like Rick, most Christians have heard a biblical principle (such as a man should leave his father and mother and cleave to his wife). But like Rick, many aren't practicing the principle. We may learn something new from a book or a sermon, but we're still not changed. Let's face it, change is hard work!

Change Is Change

We've called change different things throughout the years: discipleship, edification, sanctification, transformation, spiritual formation. These are really great terms, but they convey one simple idea: how people become more like Jesus. The early believers began to be referred to as "Christians" because of their desire to be like Christ. For simple small groups, the growth pattern is focused on how a group helps us change to become more like Jesus.

A group introduces us to something we don't already know. The members of the group challenge each other to grow in that new knowledge and put it into practice. The group encourages each member to move that growth deeply into their souls. Change continues to occur as heads and hearts are linked and our lives are transformed. Perhaps the change is a 180-degree turn as lives dramatically change. Change might be slightly less noticeable as a person makes smaller yet significant changes. Change might be movement from spiritual seeker to Christ-follower. Change can be revolutionary and mild. It all conveys the same thing: we are now different from how we once were. We are more like Jesus.

Just as with connecting, it's helpful to think of change as a continuum. We tend to consider complete transformation as the goal of change. While that would be fantastic, it's as naïve as thinking every workout routine will result in rock-hard abdominal muscles (though that would be nice!). Change can be an alteration in our thinking or a renovation of our lifestyle.

Leo and Betty hadn't been to church since they were children. Now in their early sixties, they knew very little about what it meant to be a Christian. They began attending church after some neighbors invited them to a Christmas service. Realizing they had a spiritual emptiness aching to be filled, they quickly became regular attenders. Within a few months they were invited to join a group of other grandparent-aged folks who met in a group after the early service. Leo and Betty knew nothing spiritually. They had vague recollections of childhood Bible stories, but that was it. Occasionally Leo would let slip a curse word, and Betty would discuss the recent harlequin romance novel she was reading. The group wasn't concerned about that as much as they were about helping this young-in-the-faith couple begin the change process. Forget about grand notions of complete transformation; Leo and Betty were just learning Bible stories—and changing.

We have to surrender the idea that change equals perfection. Yeah, someday, when we are with Jesus, we won't fail and our knowledge will be complete. But until then it's a process that should be surrounded with grace. We should celebrate when our group has a great discussion and when people confess and turn from sin. We should be glad they show up prepared and when they surrender more of their lives to Christ.

Getting Off Track

Groups may ambitiously plan to help members experience spiritual transformation, but two common problems can often sidetrack them: the "you-need-to-know-more" mentality and pride.

You-Need-To-Know-More

Some groups take on a materialistic approach to Bible study. They crave to know more. They may not have the same intense desire to become different people, but they sure love to dig into ancient languages, history, and cultural tidbits. Let me share one humorous example with you.

Ron and Vanessa led a group of about a dozen individuals who prized themselves on their above average spiritual IQ. The group of forty-something adults was mostly lifelong church attenders. For years they complained that the Bible studies suggested by the church "just aren't 'deep' enough." At least that's what they told Steven, the small groups pastor from their church. One evening Steven had the privilege of sitting in on the group only to discover what they considered "deep."

The Bible study was focused on a few verses from Hebrews.

> And let us consider how we may spur one another on toward love and good deeds, not giving up meeting together, as some are in the habit of doing, but encouraging one another—and all the more as you see the Day approaching.
>
> 10:24–25 TNIV

Steven was stunned when the leader, Isaac, launched into a short dissertation on the authorship of Hebrews. The leader was sure the apostle Paul wrote the letter. One of the other members of the group sharply disagreed with that assertion and quoted Martin Luther when he suggested that it was Apollos. Steven quizzically asked why it mattered, but the group ignored him.

Once the group moved past the authorship question, they spent more time on who the recipients were and where they lived. The conversation quickly shifted when one group participant asked what "the Day" referred to. Then a lively discussion erupted between those who thought it alluded to the

Rapture while others were sure it was the Day of Judgment. After that conversation cooled, the group began chasing references to "deeds" throughout Scripture and whether it was actually teaching legalism. By the end of the meeting Steven was emotionally exhausted.

After the meeting ended and the members left, Steven had a chance to interact with Isaac. "Wasn't that great?" Isaac asked.

"What do you mean?" Steven cautiously responded.

"Our deep discussion! We really got to know those verses."

"I see your point," Steven replied, searching for just the right words. "I certainly admire your passion for Scripture." Scrambling for gracious and yet challenging words, he went on, "Do you think maybe you missed some of the key elements?"

Steven feared Isaac's response, but over the next hour Steven coached the leader on the point of Bible study. It's not simply to study it like a classic poem. After all, what's the point of knowing grammar, syntax, and figures of speech if you miss the actual message? The point of Bible study is to allow the words to penetrate and change us. Isaac began to realize that the group was focused on the Bible as literature, and that the message was lost.

This may be an extreme example, but it demonstrates how a group can get sidetracked on interesting data. When a group becomes more intrigued with history, facts, and language than they are with becoming like Jesus, they have fallen into the need-to-know-more mentality.

Pride

"Everybody lies." It's one of the favorite lines of Dr. Gregory House, a fictional character from the TV series *House*. Though he is an irreligious man, he has a profound understanding of sin and brokenness. Dr. House assumes that the patients under his care are usually hiding some key to their illness and when the truth is known, they will be closer to a cure. Naturally, he's usually right.

After a twenty-year hiatus, I returned to the weight room. Since my church has a world-class exercise facility a stone's throw from my office I figured I should add some muscle-building exercises to my cardio workout. I have to be honest, I didn't remember much about increasing muscles, but I realized I'd be crazy not to make use of the well-appointed weight room. Early one Wednesday morning in the weight room, I met my friend Jim, who had offered to give me some advice and go over some basic routines. Jim is a mountain of a man with arms that proclaim he pumps iron. As Jim walked me through basic routines, my pride was slowly eroding. I wanted to tell Jim, "I'm fine. I don't really need any coaching. I know all about this equipment and what to do." But that would have been preposterous. My flabby arms would have given me away. It's still a battle with my pride. When Jason, who also lifts at the same time I do, waltzes in and bench presses fifty more pounds than I can push, my pride takes a beating. But if I want to increase my muscles, I have to surrender my pride and humbly ask for advice and guidance (and someone to spot me so I don't drop the barbell on my chest).

We do the same thing. Pride keeps members of a group from growing in a number of ways. We want to say, "I'm fine, I don't really need any coaching." We won't admit we have a problem and won't seek help. That's really funny when you think about it. We all have problems. Maybe it's a secret addiction, or just that we don't know the Bible as much as we should. We might have challenges in our marriage or with our parenting. We might not know how to handle finances or we might feel spiritually stagnant. Until we acknowledge that we need to grow and need others to help us, we will get sidetracked and will have a hard time changing.

How Does a Group Help Us Change?

So how does a group help us change? I want to suggest that God typically uses three things in a healthy group to facilitate our spiritual development. A healthy group helps each person change when we are honest, when we apply the Scriptures, and when we listen to other believers.

Honesty

We need to be real and be honest if we want to become more like Christ. If we want the group to help us with a particular sin habit, we should be able to talk about that. If we want the group to help us understand the Bible, we should be honest that we aren't biblically literate. If we are having a hard time establishing spiritual disciplines like prayer and personal Bible reading, we should ask others in the group for help. We should be honest with ourselves and with others if we want them to help us change. If we live in a community of people who hide and cover their faults, we won't be able to help them. We should invite our fellow group members to show us who they really are.

Jill was a spendaholic. She loved to spend money. Her closets (yes, she had more than one) bulged with skirts, shirts, pants, and shoes. Her work required that she dress professionally, so she reasoned that a large, sophisticated wardrobe was appropriate. While many women choose shoes that fit well, she chose footwear based on the designer. It wasn't just clothes she loved to buy. From electronics to concert tickets, Jill was a financial disaster waiting to happen. No one knew how badly into debt she was. On the surface she was a successful single professional. Her luxury sport wagon and desirable condo communicated that she had arrived. But her image was its own prison. People lavished attention on her because of the vestiges of success. What would people think if they knew she was financially leveraged and on the brink of ruin? Jill felt that she couldn't be real or her image would be ruined.

Jill is not alone. From financial problems to sexual addictions to an insatiable need to gossip to a burning resentment toward an ex-spouse, most of us have issues that we would be horrified if others knew. But as long as we hide our real issues, like Jill, we probably won't change much.

My friend Stan finally took a risk and was honest with a guy in his group. "I was tired of hiding and decided to take a risk," he explained to me. After a few months in a group with Gary, he decided to go for broke. Sitting across from Gary in an empty coffee shop, he finally asked his embarrassing question. "Do you suppose it's a sin if you have sexual fantasies about your own wife?" Stan was worried how Gary would reply. Would Gary just say, "Yes"? Would Gary quote some Scripture? Would he laugh at him? Would this ruin their developing friendship? Stan didn't care; he just wanted someone to know who he was. He was elated with Gary's instant reply.

"Man, I hope not!" In that moment the two men realized that they could talk and confess at a very deep level. They both risked rejection and began a new level of comfort with each other. From that moment on no subject was taboo or off limits.

Stan also shows us that it's not necessary for everyone in the group to know each other at the same level. His relationship with Gary produced a safe place for confession and accountability. Can you imagine if Stan had asked that same question in a couples group in front of his wife? It may have had a different outcome! However, Stan wisely pulled aside a friend within his group for a conversation.

Stan later told me that this issue, while important to him, was just a test to see if he could trust Gary. When Gary responded well, he felt it was safe to be real.

We may not be able to encourage everyone in the group to deep levels of vulnerability, but we can encourage them to be as open and honest as they are willing to be. If you hear a cliché answer, you can follow up with, "Do you really believe that or are you just repeating something you think we want to hear?" We should encourage group members to say what they truly believe.

Garry Poole, author of *Seeker Small Groups*, likes to start new groups by asking the participants, "If you could ask God one question, what would it be?" He hands out slips of paper and asks each group member to write down the question, then he spends the next several weeks of the group working through all those questions. That's one way to communicate that we are serious about talking about what's really on our minds.

I wonder how many people have great questions that they are afraid to ask. Have you wondered . . .

- If David was a man after God's own heart, why did he have a tendency to be a womanizer?
- Why does God seem nicer in the New Testament than he does in the Old?
- If God wants us to pray, why doesn't he answer my prayers?
- If God takes care of his followers, doesn't he realize that Christians in the developing world have it bad?

Those are big questions. However, most of the honest questions are closer to home.

- Can I pursue justice and a large screen LCD TV at the same time?
- Is it OK to tithe off my net income or should it be off my gross income?
- Is it materialistic to hold out for a leather interior in a car?
- Can I love people who hurt me and at the same time avoid them?

These are some of the honest questions people ask when they feel free to know and be known.

As we pursue honest questions, we are revealing who we are. We're inviting people to be honest. And as members of our community ask their questions, we are getting to know them. Not the clean version we bring out on Sunday morning for worship services, but the real one.

As I write this, I should be "honest" and say that we can have honesty in our groups at different levels. Just like Stan showed discretion and was honest with Gary, honesty doesn't mean we share every thought with every person in the group. But we can model and encourage group members to grow through honestly sharing where they are at spiritually and let them express where they would like to be.

Often it takes a group to help us be honest. Don, a good friend of mine, is a retired Air Force colonel. In the military culture a colonel is not quite like being God, but it's close. Don had served as an elder in several churches and had taught Sunday school for decades. He disdained the small groups experience because he was relationally challenged and believed the teaching outside the classroom was shallow. Ironically, he found himself a teacher for an Officer's Christian Fellowship, a small group ministry for military personnel, when he was stationed at a base in Alabama.

This particular OCF small group had as a member a rather outspoken, retired enlisted woman named Betty. This lady was relatively opinionated but well grounded in the Scripture. Don was leading the study on Romans, pontificating on the subject of grace when Betty interrupted and said matter-of-factly (but certainly not as respectfully as one would expect a staff sergeant to speak to a full colonel), "Colonel, you don't have any idea what you're talking about, do you?"

Well, in point of fact Don had a strong streak of "works" in his faith that distorted his understanding of grace. Disarmed by Betty's boldness, Don listened as she taught the teacher, providing him one of those rare "epiphanies" that God graces us with. Despite his military rank and Christian credentials, it took a subordinate in a small group setting to help him truly understand the meaning of faith. Betty helped Don become more honest.

Apply the Scriptures

Groups also help people change as they open up the Scriptures and apply them to day-to-day life. My friend Darcy was a bright, young career professional with an amazing sense of humor. She was a superb storyteller and could hold the attention of any room. But her humor had a dark side. She would often explain that her words came out before she really thought about them. Sometimes it was no big deal, but from time to time she would accidentally put others down or offend people. It bothered her, but she didn't really know what to do about the dark side of her humor.

One evening her group dove into a discussion of James 3, a text that describes the power of our words. James's letter rang in her ears. Her group was keenly aware of her quick wit and sharp tongue, but they had grown accustomed to it. Actually, the real truth was that they had learned to avoid it. For some reason, on this evening, Darcy seemed ready to surrender her mouth to Jesus.

The group was floored when she blurted out, "I've got to do something about my mouth!" Darcy went on to explain how she felt she had no control over the words that came out of her mouth. As she began to apply James 3 to her own life, she told the group she would appreciate their help. One of her friends in the group cautiously asked how she might tame her tongue. Darcy thought for a minute, then suggested to the group that she might quit watching a favorite TV show that encouraged her sarcasm. As much as she liked it, the show only fueled the darker side of her humor. Would the group be willing to ask her what she was putting into her mind? They agreed that they would.

As Darcy applied the Scripture to her life, Frank realized that he, too, should examine what was influencing his life. When it was his turn to talk, Frank thanked Darcy for her honest thoughts and confessed that he might not have the same exact issue as Darcy, but he should examine what he was putting into his mind that was coming out through some inappropriate jokes. He regularly tuned in to a radio show on the commute to work that was full of crude humor and sexual innuendos. After hearing Darcy's courageous next steps, Frank decided he was going to quit listening to the show and find something that would encourage a more Christlike life and asked if the group would be willing to ask him in the coming weeks how he was doing.

Both Frank and Darcy began to change through applying the biblical truth. At first glance this seems so obvious. Of course we should apply what we have learned, right? But a small group is one of the few places where application can be discussed. In my personal devotional time I think about ways to apply what I've read, but not as deeply as when I'm with a group. And while sermons usually contain applications, it's inappropriate in most worship services to interact with the preacher while he's on the platform speaking (in fact, in my church you will be politely escorted from the auditorium). But a group can encourage each person to ask, "How will this truth change my life?"

Listening

A few years ago I met Kent Odor at a small groups conference. As I sat in the atrium during a lull in the conference talking with Kent, I realized he wasn't an ordinary pastor. He was a brilliant thinker and well experienced in the small group world. At the time Kent was a small groups pastor at a large church in Las Vegas. I was immediately intrigued—I imagined a neon church with slot machines and very leggy ushers. I was fairly new as a small groups minister, and since he was a veteran, I asked him to be a mentor and guide, and he agreed. Over the following years I would call him and pick his brain. No matter how big or small the issue, Kent would listen as I detailed the problem. He wasn't quick to offer solutions; instead, he would probe with more questions. Only when he realized I had run out of ideas would he then begin to fill in the blanks that I couldn't quite figure out.

I began to call him "Obi-Wan" after the famous Jedi Knight from the Star Wars films. Not because he could move things with his mind, of course, but because he was a mesmerizing blend of wise sage and mystical professor. He would look at me and ask a question and no matter how I answered I knew I wouldn't be in the same ballpark. But he never made me feel small or dumb. He just kept pressing me to grow and learn—not through lectures but through listening.

Listening to one another is one of the greatest ways we can help each other change. My friend Sally found that to be very true. After a number of years with the same company she felt exhausted. She described her feelings to the other ladies in her group. She felt unappreciated for the effort she put in. She suspected a co-worker was taking credit for her work. In her view the office was more political than the Iowa caucuses leading up to an election year. Perhaps she was right, and perhaps she was wrong, but the other women listened.

As she unpacked her struggles, the other women in her group encouraged her. They reminded her that while her work was difficult, she was working for the Lord, as Paul commended in Colossians. Another woman asked if they could lay hands on her and pray for her. Afterward another woman reminded her that her self-worth wasn't attached to her career but to her relationship with Christ. And Christ considered her of significant value. As Sally listened to the members of her group share with her the truth from God's

Word, she began to adjust her attitude about work and ask Christ for a renewed heart. At first the ladies listened to her; then she listened to them.

When we listen to others, their perspective often challenges us. Chip experienced strong encouragement through a handful of simple questions. About a year earlier, he had accepted a job transfer. It was a move up in the company, and it meant he could provide better for his family. But few transitions are easy, as Chip came to realize. Eleven months into the new job, his old house still lingered on the market in Minnesota, his sons were struggling in their new school, and his wife felt isolated and abandoned by her old friends. As Chip shared his struggle with his men's group, he wondered out loud if the move was a mistake. There were sympathetic nods. Then Earl, a fairly confident older man, asked some questions. "Chip, you said months ago that you were certain God led you to this new role. Why do you doubt that now?" Chip reminded Earl of the struggles he had just shared. "So are you suggesting that following God should be without any difficulty?" Chip replied that he knew that problems were part of life. Earl finished his challenging words with, "Could it be that God has your attention in a different way during this difficult time and he wants to help you grow?" The group was stunned. But Chip knew that Earl was right. We often throw around clichés about trusting God, but trust is demonstrated primarily in the hard times. Chip was encouraged to reaffirm his own understanding of God's direction in his life. Chip's group listened to him, and then he listened to them.

This pathway of change shouldn't surprise us. The writer of Hebrews simply says, "Encourage one another" (Heb. 10:25). The writer knew there is great power in positive words that help us realize that living for Christ is possible. We can become more like him with his help and our effort. Often we want to "encourage" without knowing how our friends need to be encouraged. I know I'm quicker with my mouth than my ears. But if we want to help each other grow, it starts with the ears as we listen to each other's burdens and concerns. Then we offer the encouragement needed to help them grow.

Building the Bridge

My friend Mike loves to say, "You've got to build the relational bridge strong enough to hold the weight of truth." I love that metaphor! Imagine that a group is a series of relationships that create the foundation of the bridge, the piers, the cables, girders, and finally the roadway. Every time the group meets or members interact they add to the bridge. They secure a cable. They fasten a relational bolt. They pour cement. The more the bridge takes shape, the safer it becomes.

Have you ever received a challenging word from someone you barely knew? How well did you receive it? Or maybe it was the other extreme—a person you barely knew told you way more than you wanted to know. That happened to my friend Dennis. Over chicken sandwiches at an Irish restaurant he described a very uncomfortable conversation with Ryan. The two men had met through a mutual friend, and since they had some things in common—newly married, young professionals, working downtown—Ryan suggested they grab coffee together. Dennis, who is a quiet man, agreed. Within several minutes of their meeting Ryan told Dennis that he struggled with sexual addiction and Internet porn and wanted Dennis to join an accountability group with him.

"I felt bad," Dennis said, blushing, "but I barely knew him. He dumped way too much personal information on me! I told him I was too busy." Dennis was confused. He didn't know why the idea churned in him so badly. Then Mike's metaphor hit me.

"He didn't build the relational bridge." Essentially, Ryan wanted Dennis to help him change. But there was no relational trust yet. They hadn't even decided to build a bridge yet and Ryan was ready to start driving a semi truck across it.

As we lead our groups, we can help our members change as we build the relational bridge. The next chapter explores specific ways we can help our people become more like Jesus.

.

5

the nuts and bolts of changing

Helping People Become More Christlike

Overwhelmed by Change

The whole idea of change is overwhelming. Can we really help the people in our group change? Most of us have a hard enough time changing ourselves! Our basements are museums of exercise equipment that were going to change our appearance, and instead they air-dry our clothes. After a week on the low-carb diet we blow it over a dozen glazed donuts at Krispy Kreme. It might be that we look at change with trepidation because we have been going about it all wrong. We are trying to change too much, too soon, with no help.

When business journalist Alan Deutschman began researching how people successfully changed, he bumped into a startling reality: people change more consistently and stay changed through relationships! Through his research he discovered three simple concepts that helped people change:

1. A new relationship or community of people provides inspiration and hope that change is possible

2. The community helps each person learn, practice, and master the new habits and skills that are needed for successful change
3. The new community helps create a new way of looking at the world

In his book *Change or Die*, Deutschman explored change success stories about heart attack patients, paroled ex-convicts, and angry factory workers. Each group of people changed from self-destructive lifestyles to healthy habits. The consistent factor was community. When people connected with a community that helped them, change was possible. Without the community people rarely changed, and when they did, it didn't last. The change wasn't instantaneous, but over time people were transformed.

As we lead our groups, we should be confident that each member has great potential for change. As the group discusses what it means to follow Jesus in every corner of life, they are learning new skills. The community of believers can help redefine how we see the world. Just like us, the people in our groups won't change overnight. But as the group journeys together, most members will come out of the experience different people.

The Change Continuum

Just like the relational pattern of connecting, the growth pattern of change is a continuum. Some groups will help their members change in huge ways. They will see bad habits broken and good ones form. Or they might see the spiritual light flicker on for the first time in a participant. "Change" is simply movement toward Christ.

We need to resist defining change as perfection. That's a standard none of us can attain. Sure, some people have dramatic transformations. Just like some people can quit smoking in one day while others need a month of patches and nicotine gum. In my experience most people are patch and gum people. It doesn't mean they are weak. Just like a fitness program starts slow and builds, a group will often see small improvements that grow. When a woman learns humility in grace through a discussion of Philippians, that's change. When a college student confesses his foul mouth and quits using R-rated swear words, that's change. I'd like us to look at three points along the change continuum: learn, grow, and transform.

Learn

Learning occurs when we hear a truth that we didn't know before. Perhaps we're introduced to a section of Scripture or a principle from the Bible for the first time. Perhaps the group reads a section from the Bible and then discusses what it meant thousands of years ago to the people who first read it. Then discussion moves to what the words might mean for us today.

This is a very important stage. Particularly early in faith when everything is new, learning things previously un-known is exciting. Let me introduce you to a couple in their midthirties, Kelley and Paul. When Kelley and Paul began attending their group they felt a little nervous. They were new Christians and admittedly knew very little. But their group was geared just for them. The leader of the group took a little more time teaching before the discussion. Sometimes they watched a thirty-minute video featur-ing a skilled teacher. Paul described himself as a sponge just soaking it all up. Kelley described herself as "clueless" when it came to how to read the Bible. But as the group continued to meet, they began to learn all sorts of new things.

Groups that focus primarily on learning often have an academic quality to them. Many are classroom based. They may rely on a skilled teacher to bring a lesson to the group. Since most people in the learning phase are curious about the Scriptures and biblical truth, they thirst for more information. While they might risk getting sidetracked on the "you-need-to-know-more" path, learning meets the needs of people who just "need-to-know." The big question during the learning phase is, "What does this mean?"

Grow

The growing phase is perceptible when the emphasis shifts from new learning to application of the truth. The group members become preoccupied with living out the truth they are learning.

Let's check back with Paul and Kelley. Their group gathers every other Thursday night to discuss what the Bible says about marriage in Ephesians 5. Paul felt challenged to put into practice the writings of the apostle Paul and love his wife at least as much as he loved himself. And his regular hunting trips, nice car, and fishing boat give ample evidence of his self-love. When the group reconvened two weeks later, Kelley reported that Paul cancelled a fishing trip and took her out for coffee for the first time in months. It may be a small sprout, but Paul is growing.

A group helps a person grow by challenging each person in the group to apply truth and then encouraging it when they see it in action. The big question in the growing phase is, "How does this impact the way I live?"

Transform

The next phase of change is transforming. While we won't be fully transformed until we are united with God, we can experience transformation in select areas of our lives. While some sins may haunt us for many years, others persist because we lack a community to help us overcome them.

Kelley had a temper. While it might be more common for men to get angry more than women, Kelley could keep up with the best of them. One week en route to the small group meeting she was even given a ticket for an incidence of "road rage" when she caused a minor accident after tailgating someone who had cut her off. After apologizing to the group for being late and explaining what had happened, she proclaimed, "It just makes me so mad! Some people should not be allowed to drive!" Later that evening, one of the other women took her aside and timidly suggested she read Colossians 3:8, which says, "But now you must rid yourselves of all such things as these: anger, rage, malice, slander, and filthy language from your lips." She hadn't considered that the Bible had something to say about the way she drove!

Her change was gradual at first. She would apologize to her husband and co-workers after she had a blowup. Then after a couple of months she happily reported that she hadn't even yelled for two weeks. Her husband concurred that she was much more patient and quick to forgive, even when he was clearly in the wrong. Is Kelley completely transformed? No, but in that one area she has experienced some transforming work.

When members of the group put effort toward transforming, they become more aware of the areas of life that need to be yielded to God. Often people in this phase become engaged in what many call spiritual disciplines. Perhaps they journal, fast, and dedicate time to prayer. Some would refer to this pursuit as growing more "intimate" with Christ. Far from judgmental or arrogant, transforming groups are more aware of their own sin and need to yield to Christ. They inspire the people around them to grow deeper with Christ. The big question in the transforming phase is, "Who am I becoming?"

Where Is Your Group?

Before you move on to the specific things you can do to help the members of your group change, explore these questions and attempt to identify which phase of change your group is at.

- Is most of your group time spent on completing a Bible study?
- Do most of your members get upset if the group time is cut short for prayer or discussion?
- Do you primarily use videos during group time?

If you answered yes to all of these, you are likely in the learning phase of change.

- Do your group members openly discuss areas in which they need to personally grow?
- Do people in your group share stories of success and failure as they attempt to live for Christ?
- Do your members ask to be held accountable for their actions?
- Do members confess their sins to each other?

If you answered yes to all of these, you are likely in the growing phase of change.

- Do group members point to areas where they feel they have experienced victory over a sin or bad habit?
- Can the group affirm noticeable areas of change?
- Do members discuss their spiritual disciplines?

If you answered yes to all of these, you are likely in the transforming phase of change.

What Can You Do to Help the Group Members Change during the Learn Phase?

Learn Together

When a group is full of new Christians, it's important to pick a tool that makes learning simple and enjoyable. If it's complicated and difficult, they may abandon the effort. Some groups learn together by picking a Bible study that focuses on the simpler stories from the Bible. Narratives about the life of Jesus, the early church, and some from the Old Testament will introduce people to foundational topics of faith without requiring that they know much about the Bible.

If your group wants to tackle a tougher subject and as the leader you don't feel up to that challenge, you may want to invite a teacher for a season. This is helpful when a leader is unsure of her or himself. One church uses "living resources." These resources are experts on particular subjects. A group can invite the expert to teach the group over several weeks. Other groups use videos of skilled teachers who help teach more difficult subjects. When a group learns together, they enter a joint journey that celebrates new knowledge.

Memorize Scripture Together

The psalmist said, "I have hidden your word in my heart that I might not sin against you" (Ps. 119:11). Much later, the apostle Paul wrote, "All Scripture is inspired by God and is useful to teach us what is true and to make us realize what is wrong in our lives. It corrects us when we are wrong and teaches us to do what is right. God uses it to prepare and equip his people to do every good work" (2 Tim. 3:16–17 NLT). Whether your group is full of people at the starting place of faith or long-term believers, it's a great habit to memorize Scripture together.

We often think of Scripture memory as something children should do. But the Word of God has a transforming ability. Of all literature it uniquely has a track record of producing change. However, memorizing Scripture often requires some motivation. Groups that memorize together often will pick helpful passages and then recite them together at some point during the group. Scripture memory is helpful at each phase of change but can be particularly helpful during the learn phase.

Make It a Matter of Prayer

A meaningful time of prayer can help each member grow. We struggle to understand how prayer motivates God, changes us, and helps us understand God in our lives. And yet it is one of the most significant parts of the spiritual life. In a well-guided time of sharing prayer requests, people will often confess sins or discuss areas where they would like to grow.

When a group turns to prayer time, they share what's really happening in life. As the group wrapped up their discussion, Ernie asked the group if there were any prayer requests. Darcy and Greg asked for prayer as they had begun marriage counseling. The group was stunned. No one knew the couple was struggling in their relationship. But the prayer time gave them an opportunity to be open. It's not the sort of thing a couple will likely blurt out over coffee at the beginning of the gathering or in the middle of a Bible discussion. Most people need a time to share those personal matters. If you want to have a great prayer time, you should consider these three things.

First, keep it small. A group larger than twelve people is just too big for most people to openly share thoughts, concerns, and struggles. Most people don't want to take up everyone else's time. Or they are too shy to express their concerns and issues. If you lead a large group, consider splitting up in groups of four or six for prayer time. If it's a mixed group, split along gender lines or pair couples together. I would recommend that you keep the same prayer partners for at least a few months so that people become more comfortable with each other. Perhaps they will be more inclined to share what's really going on in their lives.

Second, give it time. Leave enough time for people to share prayer requests. If your group meets for two hours, leave at least twenty or thirty minutes for people to talk about their concerns or issues. Remember the math: if each person talks for five minutes, how long will it take to hear each person? If you don't break into small groups for prayer, it will take an hour for a group of twelve people to each share their prayer requests.

Third, guide it well. If you are leading a new group, suggest that participants offer prayer requests for personal things they really want the group to remember in prayer. That will probably remove prayer requests for a co-worker's distant cousin's pet, or anything else that the person isn't deeply in prayer about. It helps when you model this as a leader.

Prayer may seem like a funny way to help us change. But a huge part of change is looking to God for his guidance and support. Most of the issues we ask for prayer (health, careers, family, fertility) are all opportunities to grow to become like Jesus. How we respond in difficulty is a common theme throughout Scripture, and from Moses to David, God did some of his finest change work when men and women went to him in prayer. A group can remind us of that reality each time we set aside several minutes for focus on God.

What Can You Do to Help the Group Members Change during the Growing Phase?

Discuss the Bible

Bible study has been a common feature in small groups for many years. However, I wonder if the term is helpful.

I've attended many things under the label "Bible study." One Bible study was a large event held in a church auditorium with a teacher and rows of learners. Of the seventy or so people in attendance, few interacted with the lecturer. Another Bible study I attended included a stack of resources including a Bible dictionary and handbook, a concordance, and a handful of commentaries. The group was divided into teams and explored everything from ancient customs to language and grammar. Toward the end of the study we joined together again, and each group reported what they had learned. A different Bible study involved a twenty-five-minute DVD followed by printed questions the group answered. Another type of Bible study gathered a handful of older men early on a Wednesday morning. They read a passage of Scripture followed by a short devotional, then listed the prayer concerns of the church. All four of these were called Bible studies, but each clearly describes very different approaches to interacting with the Scriptures in a group setting. The term "study" might not be the most helpful.

But when a healthy group *discusses* the Scriptures, the members explore what the text meant thousands of years ago to the original audience and what it means to us today. The Bible is described as a living organism, a sword that performs surgery, and a guiding light.[1] The extraordinary thing about the Bible is that a woman with a PhD can be changed by the words just as can the man who is working toward his GED. It does not require a college degree in theology to be able to discuss the Scriptures.

A good discussion requires two components. The first is an exploration of the author's intended message. This is determined by looking at the context around the passage and by inquiring who the original audience was. The second key component for the discussion is applying it to life. This should be personal, not just theoretical. If it was a mathematical equation, it might look like this:

meaning of passage (context + original audience)
+
personal application
=
good discussion

Some groups find printed curriculum a great help discussing the Bible. They follow the flow of the questions and use it to interact with one another. However, other groups benefit by simply picking a book of the Bible, reading a section together, making observations about the context, and then talking about how it applies to life. I'm not a stickler for terms, so if you really like "study," use that instead of "discussion." I would simply recommend that whatever term you find most comfortable, you digest biblical truth together and encourage one another to apply it to life.

Mirror Time

Probably the most anxiety-producing pathway toward helping us change is confrontation. No one wants to be confronted. And no one wants to confront. Yes, there are some odd people out there who love to confront. They are scary people and probably should be confronted for liking confronting others. But aside from that fraction of people, most of us don't like it.

My friend Bill Donahue tried to soften it by calling it "carefrontation."[2] While the term may induce giggles, it probably better expresses the intent of the action than any other term. In carefrontation we care enough about the person and their spiritual well-being to talk to them about the truth. But we approach them tenderly, as a friend who cares, not as a crusader of truth. Carefrontation might help us clarify how we should approach this delicate pathway to change. On at least two occasions in the New Testament we are taught how to help others when they are stuck doing what they shouldn't do (Matt. 18:15–17; Gal. 6:1–2). In those two sections of Scripture, Jesus, and later Paul, teach humility and compassion. We talk to them about what we observe. We hope for change.

Let's be honest: we're not always the carefronters—sometimes we need the carefrontation. We also need a community of people to help us grow. We need friends who will have the courage to pursue us when we are heading down a path that will lead us away from Christ. We are often better at identifying the problems others have than we are at identifying our own. In fact, Jesus taught about this problem. He pointed out that ironically, we are able to see a small sliver in the eye of another person and yet we don't notice the log in our own eye (Matt. 7:1–5). I think Jesus was trying to make us laugh at the paradox. It's almost humorous that I can see the smallest defect in another person and will leave my own issues unaddressed. Since it's a problem we all share, we all need trusted members of a community to help show us what needs to change.

I think what we need is *mirror time.* Have you ever walked through a clothing store and been surprised by a mirror? You pass by and something catches your eye. You stop and look, and there you are in a full-length mirror. You are horrified at what you see. You quickly straighten out your shirt or your hair. You stand up straight. The mirror caught you when you weren't ready—and it's disturbing. Disheveled or frumpy, slouching posture or protruding paunch, we don't like the person we see in the mirror. We wish for distorted mirrors from the circus that make us look thinner or taller.

What we actually need is more mirror time like that. Not to check out our physical appearance. No, what we need are friends from our group who will hold up the mirror and simply ask, "Do you like who you see?" And we need to be willing to prop up the mirror for our friends and be willing to ask them the same question.

While driving down a busy street on our way to a retreat, Susan asked me, "What does the 'Lord of Hosts' mean?" She had been reading the Bible on her own and was puzzled by the term.

"I usually suggest people do their own Bible studies!" I blurted back, trying to be funny. As an amateur comedian, I'm prone toward botched attempts at humor.

"Ouch," Susan responded.

It took a minute for me to realize that I had hurt Susan's feelings. I had not meant to be unkind; I was trying to be funny. Susan's "ouch" held up the mirror as if to ask, "Is the need to be funny more important than the feelings of others?"

We can use the mirror like that. We don't have to always overthink our words, plan a conversation, and share a well-crafted speech. Sometimes we should hold up the mirror and simply ask, "Did you mean to say that?" Many of us with children try to teach them to use words to express their feelings. If a sibling takes something, politely ask for it to be returned. If they hurt feelings, tell them how it made you feel. But as we get older we tend to bury those thoughts and only express them when the offender is not around. I would not have had a growth opportunity if Susan had bottled up the hurt. I would have figured the joke was a dud. It wouldn't have occurred to me that it was a missile. A little mirror provided a lot of growth.

Sometimes it's appropriate to think through how to best use the mirror. There are times when we do need to craft the words so that we can elicit the best chance for change. John did just that when he started his conversation with Liam. "Do you know that after our small group, Rachel drives home to her apartment in tears?"

Liam was surprised by John's question. He liked Rachel and didn't have any idea there was a problem. Though the group had only been meeting about six months, they were already forming close bonds with one another. Liam and

John had become good friends through the group, and John figured it was important to talk with his friend about this. Liam had one huge blind spot—he talked too much. Whatever Liam was thinking he shared. Everyone in the group participated in the discussion, but Liam was the word king— he spoke far more than anyone else. Occasionally someone would tell him he talked too much, but he reasoned that he had a lot to say because he knew so much.

Liam was stunned when John went on to explain that Rachel was so upset because she felt that Liam monopolized the conversation and she was tired of competing just to get a word in. John asked Liam what he thought and how he could help his friend use fewer words in the gathering. He helped Liam realize that growing in Christ is linked to serving others and focusing on their needs. If he could serve Rachel by encouraging her to talk and if he could discipline his mouth, he would mature as a friend (and as a follower of Christ).

Until that moment Liam didn't think he had a talking problem. People teased him about his verbosity, but he took it more as a compliment. "I thought I was 'social' or a 'conversationalist,'" Liam later explained to me. John held up the mirror for Liam and asked him if he liked the person he saw. He didn't. Liam credits that tough conversation as a key moment that helped him change to be like Christ. He knew that the tongue was a powerful instrument. He knew the Bible cautions us in speech. But it wasn't until someone held up the mirror that he realized he had to apply the biblical principles to his life. Liam told me, "I still talk too much, but I slow down and at times just hold my breath in a group so I don't monopolize the conversation."

Holding up the mirror is hard. Looking in the mirror is hard. But doing it in the company of people who love us makes it easier. A group should first discuss the value of mirror time and receive permission from each other. The relational bridge should be built strong enough to hold the image in the mirror. Probably the first few months a group is together should be "mirror free." But as a group builds trust, the mirror should be welcome. I know that I respond to the mirror better when I have confidence that the person holding it is trying to help me and not trying to put me down.

It's also important that the group not "gang up on" a single individual. Rather, just as it can be more effective to break into smaller prayer groups, it may be better for the leader to encourage "mirror time" to occur in a smaller group or even individually outside of group time, just as with John and Liam.

What Can You Do to Help the Group Members Change during the Transforming Phase?

Set Personal Spiritual Goals

Groups can help each member set and maintain personal spiritual goals. When Doug joined my group, he came with one request: "Please encourage me to read my Bible." Those may not have been his exact words, but it was obvious that he wanted the guys in our group to encourage him to stay plugged in to the Scriptures. It became a topic of conversation at each group meeting. A couple of weeks later Doug purchased a small Bible with daily readings arranged so that the whole Bible would be read in one year. He loved it. The group encouraged him to keep reading, and then the rest of us caught his enthusiasm.

Soon all the men in the group had a one-year Bible. We didn't guilt anyone into maintaining the goal. Instead, like runners in a race we encouraged each other to keep going. It worked. For most of the guys it produced the most faithful Bible reading that any of us had previously experienced. We celebrated together when we remained faithful to the calendar and shared what we had read that week. As we read the Scriptures regularly, we made new spiritual discoveries that helped us grow in Christ.

Setting personal goals encourages each person to take more control of their spiritual development. Let's be honest, we usually give about an hour a week in a worship service and about two hours every other week in a small group and figure that will grow us spiritually. We know that won't really cut it, but that's the extent of the effort that many people make.

One way to help members at this phase set goals might be to have a special goal-setting meeting. Encourage each person to come prepared with a list of two or three areas they would like the group to help them work on. The goals might be reading the Scripture regularly or keeping a prayer journal. For another their goal might be using their spiritual gifts and serving others. And others in the group might ask for prayer and support as they notch up their missional efforts at work by having spiritual conversations with friends there. I would recommend that the goals be measurable. A goal such as "I'd like to improve to be a better Christian" is too subjective for the goal maker or the group members to recognize success.

Confession

At the end of my freshman year of college I applied to be an RA, a student who was responsible for a whole floor of the residence hall. Truth be told, the real reason I wanted the job was so that I could have my own room and a little extra cash. Of course, I never told the people interviewing me that. I remember one question the interviewer asked me all those years ago: "Name one or two weakness you have."

Like I'm going to tell you, I thought to myself. I quickly scrambled for the answer, still trying to look confident. I couldn't tell him the truth—that I gazed probably too longingly at some of my female classmates. Nor could I tell him

I can be pretty self-centered. Fortunately a safe confession came to me just in the nick of time. "I care too much!" I stridently confessed. I don't think he bought it. At least he didn't offer me the job.

Let's face it, confession is terrifying! Sure, it can help us grow in many helpful and rewarding ways. But most of us fear how others will react to our confession, which keeps us from being truly open. We take a huge risk when we confess in a group. What we share might become public information or we might lose credibility with the members of our group. At least that's what we think. And for good reason. Some of us have been betrayed while others of us have lost friendships. Still others have friends who want to hear our confession, then fix our ailment so we never sin again.

It's unfortunate we are not more comfortable with confession. My friend John, a counselor at a state university, says that psychologists are the priests of the modern era. He has said that he thinks people go to their therapist to confess sin and seek absolution. John wonders if the need for counselors would be as great if people confessed sins to friends. We need to confess our faults far more that we realize. Our mental health is at stake!

James, the half-brother of Jesus, knew that a healthy spiritual life included the confession of sin. What's interesting is that he didn't tell us to confess our sins to God. Instead, he encouraged us to confess our sins to each other and pray for each other (James 5:17). Think about that. One of the men who knew Jesus better than perhaps any other human, who grew up with him in the same home, who was probably more familiar with his teaching than even Peter or John, told us that we should confess our sins to each other! We almost never talk about this! We suggest that Christians confess their sins to God in prayer, not to each other. Yet, for us to become more like Christ, confession should be part of our practice. If I were into conspiracy theories I might suggest that the devil would rather we never confess our sins to each other because we might actually change to become more like Jesus.

Let me give you some simple confession tips. First, confirm that what is said in the group should stay in the group. Gossip will destroy confession. Second, make sure the relational bridge is strong enough. If the group isn't ready to hear the confession, it will be very awkward. Third, lead by example. If you want to introduce this into your group, model how it should be done. Finally, don't solve the confessor's problem unless they ask for help. Nothing squelches confession like a room full of unsolicited advice.

Confession is more likely to occur in smaller groups that are made up of one gender. A man is less likely to talk about struggles with sexual purity in a couples group. However, a gathering of four or five men should welcome such confession. A group of couples can either encourage more general confession, such as struggles with financial contentment, or they could split by gender for a portion of the meeting to encourage confession and more intimate prayer.

Summary

One of my favorite TV shows is *The Biggest Loser*. When it first aired on TV, I thought the idea exploited extremely overweight people. Then I got sucked in to the stories. Participants had struggled throughout their lives with weight problems. They knew they needed to change, but they couldn't do it on their own. Through great personal coaching and a supportive community they began to learn new eating skills, exercise routines, and attitudes. During the first several weeks the small changes that each person makes don't produce much change. One person loses five pounds and another eleven. But the change isn't noticeable. At the end of the season the weigh-in show displays the dramatic results of all those small efforts toward change.

When we talk about the pattern of change, let's free ourselves from the fantasy that we can help people quit sinning, completely understand complicated doctrine, live contentedly, and master all the spiritual disciplines in four weeks or less! Instead, let's celebrate each small effort that leads to a life focused more on Jesus.

Reflection

Before moving on to the next pattern, take a few moments and reflect on these questions.

1. Read Hebrews 10:24–25. How can your group "spur" each other on?

2. How has your current group (or past group experiences) helped you change? What things have you tried to change on your own? How has that worked out?

3. Do you agree that many people get off track spiritually? Why or why not?

105

4. Has your group built a relational bridge strong enough to hold the weight of truth? If not, how can you build relational trust (connect) while helping people grow (change)?

5. Of the three phases of change (learn, grow, transform), where is your group? What leads you to this conclusion?

6. Assuming your group wants to, how can you challenge your group to take the next step of changing? What will you try to get them there?

cultivating

The Missional Pattern

cul * ti * vate [kuhl-tuh-veyt]

The process of helping each group member
serve others and share their faith.

6

the pattern of cultivating

The Way Groups Revolutionize the World

Most of us who lead groups are quite comfortable with the idea that we should help our people connect and change. But encourage our group members to serve and share their faith? Now that doesn't seem like something groups are good at, or should even try. At least that's what I used to think.

Mike and Sheila asked the living room full of couples if we were willing to invite Julie to our group. The room was silent, not because we were an unwelcoming bunch, but because of Julie's circumstances. Married less than two years, Julie had recently discovered that her husband was cheating on her. He was completely unrepentant and unwilling to work on their broken marriage, even though she was willing. Mike and Sheila suggested that our community could help her through this difficult time. She was new to our area; she knew few people besides Sheila, whom she worked with. Perhaps, our leaders suggested, our group could take on the mission of helping a person in need.

I remember thinking (and then saying), we're a couples group, and we wouldn't have anything in common. How could a group of couples help her? Wouldn't hanging out with a bunch of happily married couples depress her even more? I think I secretly didn't want a needy person to be an emotional drain on our group. I wanted to preserve a little personal Switzerland where I could have peace and tranquility. I was a pastor of a church and figured I deserved a neutral zone that would be free from this sort of effort. Besides all of that, our group had finally bonded relationally and this new wrinkle would mess it up.

Would we cultivate missional lives and care for another person, or would we focus more on ourselves? Our group voted, and thanks to my pushing, she was not invited to join us. At the time, it seemed like the right decision. Ironically, our budding community didn't last very long after that. Each couple went their separate way. To this day I think the reason our group tanked was because I focused us too far inward without any concern for those outside.

Let's face it, when it comes to small groups, we can do pretty well with connecting and changing, but we stink at cultivating missional lives. We will throw ten parties and social events, and serve together as a group once a year (or less). We will spend hours in discussions about the Bible and less than fifteen minutes talking to someone outside of our community about faith in Jesus Christ. This is a problem we can't ignore. Jesus said there's a lot of work to do and we should pray that God would send people to help others (Matt. 9:35–38) and he said everyone should be prepared to share their faith and help others grow spiritually (Matt. 28:19–20). Paul said God gives spiritual gifts to all believers so they can help others (1 Cor. 12:7). Jesus's half-brother, James, wrote that faith is demonstrated in how we help others with their physical needs (2:14–17). Only focusing inward on our own needs and the needs of our little community is not an option.

There are days I wonder what would've happened to our group if I had realized the need for the missional pattern. If we had taken in a person in need, would our group have grown closer? Would we have galvanized around the desire to care for her? Would we have better understood the need to live holy, God-honoring lives? How would Julie have been affected? Would she have flourished in a community of love and acceptance after the brutality of abandonment? Would her image of the church been altered from a sixty-minute worship service to a family of friends? Perhaps her marriage could have been salvaged if a community also pursued her husband. We'll never really know.

What Does It Mean to Cultivate?

Cultivating missional lives means that we serve others and share our faith. It means that we demonstrate, through lives of service, our love for Jesus. Sometimes cultivating is when we use our spiritual gifts to build up believers, sometimes cultivating is when we share the gospel message, and sometimes cultivating is when we simply take care of the physical needs of a person going through a hardship. Clear and simple, cultivating is formed through gazing outside of our group and not inward. It comes alive when a group helps each member keep a look outside of their community for those who need God's love. Missional living means that we are focused on the "mission" of loving those outside of our community as Jesus loves them.

Groups that are good at cultivating often live outside of their comfort zone. They inconvenience themselves by focusing more on others than on themselves. And ironically, this outward focus can help build an even stronger inward community because the comfort of self-focus can actually be an enemy of true community! Alan Hirsch said it well in *Forgotten Ways.*

111

The most vigorous forms of community are those that come together in the context of a shared ordeal or those that define themselves as a group with a mission that lies beyond themselves—thus initiating a risky journey. Too much concern with safety and security, combined with comfort and convenience, has lulled us out of the true calling and purpose.[1]

We know it's true. Military veterans will tell you that it is true. Once you share a mission that places you shoulder to shoulder, you will build a tighter bond than you typically will in a circle. Sixty years after World War II, veterans groups still rent hotel conference rooms to reunite with men from a community that shared a common mission. Groups that embrace the mantle of mission will be stronger than groups that amp up just their connecting energy.

I love the term *cultivate*. It's so hopeful. It's a process term and not an end. You're never done cultivating. There's always something new to cultivate. It's a great farm word. Imagine the farmer on his tractor tilling soil in the early spring. As he turns over acres of dirt he dreams of the corn and green beans that will someday sprout. He wonders about the rain. Will there be enough? Will there be too much? After tilling the earth it's time for the fertilizer and weed prevention. Then the seed. We take it for granted, but that little seed in the earth is a miracle. At just the right time a sliver of green pokes through the soil. As the farmer watches the vegetation grow he looks for indicators of a healthy crop. He keeps an eye out for insects that might steal his work. Perhaps he supplements nature and irrigates during the dry time. When the vegetables are ripe, he harvests and sends his produce to market. And then he returns to the soil to cultivate it for the next season. When is a farmer done cultivating? I don't think he is ever finished.

We're never done cultivating missional lives in our groups. We can always study how Jesus served others. We can explore spiritual gifts. We can serve together as a group. We can help each member explore their unique personality and calling and help them live a missional life in their work, school, and neighborhood. It's a generative process that we can grow in each participant in our community. It is, in fact, the Christian life.

How Do Groups Help Us Cultivate?

Small groups have a unique ability to help each member develop the missional pattern. Groups can live out this value, but often the group serves as counselor, cheerleader, and supporter for the cultivating lifestyle that each individual lives on their own. Let me liberate you from thinking that serving or evangelism is something that a group must do together for it to count. It's fine for a group to do those things together, but most of the time our groups help each member do those things on their own. Groups can help each person cultivate in unique ways.

Let me be clear: the pattern of cultivating does not mean your group stops by the orphanage every Thursday to play with the kids, swings into the shelter on Friday to cook and lead worship, and wakes up early Sunday to hold babies in the church nursery just before you all go teach Sunday school. Cultivating missional lives is not an event but a way of life. The group engages each member to keep an open ear and eye to watch for ways to serve and testify for Christ in work, home, neighborhood, and school. That may sound tough, but it really isn't. I'll go into simple steps to help your group cultivate in the next chapter. In the meantime let's explore how a group helps build the cultivating pattern.

Break the Ice: Softening Hard Hearts

I wish the longer I attended church and called myself a Christian, the more I would have a heart for the world around me. Instead, like most Christians, I find myself in a safe little cocoon surrounded by Christian friends, who listen to inoffensive music, which I can purchase from a Christian bookstore, along with my Christian fiction, inspirational, and leadership books. I talked with one guy who said how much he'd like to work at a church so he wouldn't have to work around people who swear and live immoral lives! It's too easy to get cut off from the "real world" and develop an apathetic heart for people who have real needs.

That is exactly what my friend Charlie would say. "I hated telling people I was a pastor. It always made them jumpy." He used to frequent a discount hairstylist, the kind of shop where you were unlikely to see the same stylist twice. It seemed that Charlie always got the stylists who liked to talk. Before they knew that he was a minister they would confess their life's issues. They would go into graphic detail about the no-good boyfriend who they finally kicked out of their apartment. Or the great new boyfriend who had just moved in. They described the wild parties they attended recently. Or they would recommend the best new place to find a great martini. All along Charlie would pray, *God, please don't let them ask me what I do for a living!* But inevitably it would come up. Abruptly the conversation would become uncomfortable. The stylist would become embarrassed that they had just told a "priest" their sins. "I always stumble with how to reply. Do I tell them about Jesus? Do I tell them that I don't judge them? Or they should live a more decent life? Or come to my church?" Charlie questioned.

I can relate to Charlie. At about the same time as his string of barbershop confessions, my wife and I took a trip with our three-month-old daughter to Florida. Karyn's younger sister also came with us. On the return flight the plane had three seats on one side and two on the other. Since there were four of us, I graciously offered the three continuous seats to the ladies. Selfishly I was hoping to quietly read while seated next to the young stranger beside me.

During the preflight preparation the flight attendant played a video to explain how a seat belt works (does anyone really not know this?). The video was preceded with a little light jazz music. As the soundtrack to the video began, the guy next to me rocked a little in his seat and ribbed me with his elbow and quietly exclaimed, "Sounds like porno music!" Now, I don't want to sound like a prude, but I didn't know that genre of film had its own soundtrack. I replied with raised eyebrows and a weak smile and a shrug, hoping that would be the end of our conversation. It wasn't.

For the next hour and fifty-five minutes he would interrupt my reading to tell me more about his life. He told me that he had recently been expelled from college because according to the administration he had a "drinking problem" (he made air quotation marks as he said "drinking problem"). He missed the fraternity but not the school and was returning from Florida after some great partying. I began to pray that God would keep him from asking me *the* question. During the last fifteen minutes of the flight he popped the terrifying question, "So what do you do for a living?" Trying to downplay it, I told him that I was "on staff" at a church. I was hoping he'd think I was a janitor and leave it at that. He looked puzzled. "What do you mean?" he asked. "Are you a priest?" As I attempted to explain what I did at the church, he grew more and more uncomfortable. I didn't say a word about his movie watching or drinking habits. I tried to say as few words as possible.

I'm sure smarter, godlier people than I would have had just the right words at that moment, but I choked. I thought perhaps early on I should have talked about church or God and thus signal the would-be confessor to not be so honest about his life. I fumbled the ball. I figured it wasn't my fault that I didn't know how to steer the conversation and had the right to bail out.

As Charlie and I swapped stories of good witnessing gone bad over coffee at our local Starbucks, our third friend, Jon, who was also a pastor, suggested we had a deeper problem. He wondered out loud if we had hard hearts toward needy people. It's not that we were judgmental. We were just uncompassionate and avoidant. When Jon suggested we just didn't care, we tried to come up with better explanations for our lack of grace. But we were stuck; we might not have said any words of judgment, but our lack of words communicated it nonetheless.

I've read books on evangelism. I've heard sermons on evangelism. I went to a Bible college and took a course for an entire semester called "Personal Evangelism." But I didn't ever come to grips with my hard heart until a trusted friend held up the mirror and asked if I was looking at a person who really cared about broken people. It's not that the books, sermons, or class were a waste. They were important pieces of my development, but that little community with Charlie and Jon challenged me to break the ice and soften my heart toward those in need of Jesus.

Jesus encouraged us to focus more on the needs of others than ourselves. He challenged his followers to live a *self-less* life, not a *self-ish* one. "For whoever wants to save his life will lose it, but whoever loses his life for me will find it" (Matt. 16:25). Unfortunately, our tendency is to focus on ourselves and develop a frosty edge that pushes out the needs of others. A community that develops the cultivating lifestyle will remind us that Jesus loves the wandering sheep. We can prompt each other that our love for God will be shown in how we pursue those who have wandered away from him (Ezek. 34:1–16). A group can chip away at the ice that forms around our hearts and remind us to love the people God places in our path. But warming our hearts is just one way a group helps us cultivate. We need to get involved too.

They Is You: Get in the Game

Do you remember the term *inertia* from high school physics? It is the simple principle that an object in motion stays in motion and an object at rest stays at rest. I think we are often trapped by our own inertia. When it comes to cultivating missional lives, if we are not involved in serving and sharing our faith already, it's hard to get started. And if we are serving and sharing, maintaining motion is easier and more natural. So if you're at rest, how do you get started?

I think one major reason we don't get involved is we think someone else will take care of it. Whether it's a co-worker's broken heart or the widow three doors down, we figure someone will take care of them. How many times have you heard, "They ought to get someone to take care of that?" "That" may refer to litter alongside the road, an empty food pantry at a shelter, or the church children's ministry that is woefully understaffed. Sometimes we hear or see the need and think, *Someone ought to do something about that.*

That attitude used to drive my old senior pastor, Jeff, crazy. Ironically, *we* are usually a huge part of the solution to most problems. But we would rather have someone else take care of the inconvenience. During one talk with ministry leaders Jeff challenged us to quit looking for some mysterious "they" to take care of things. If we saw a Styrofoam cup blowing around the parking lot, go pick it up. Don't wait for the custodian to see it and retrieve it. To underline his point he coined the term "They is you." The phrase stuck with me all these years later. One thing we can do in our groups is encourage everyone to think of themselves as solutions to the problems at work, in their homes, and neighborhoods. *They is you.*

Invariably someone in your group will begin to share a burden (or a complaint). As they talk about their passion and concern for an issue, they usually are hoping someone else will take up the mantle and do something about it. As members of your group discuss feuding neighbors, the friend

cultivating

at work whose marriage is falling apart, or the classmate who is drinking too much, we can remind them that God is placing these issues before them as an invitation to get involved. Sometimes these topics come out during prayer time as well as in general conversation. Instead of giving a nod and a grimace, we can remind our fellow group members that God might want them to be part of the solution. Instead of hoping someone else will bring peace in the neighborhood, or help the co-worker, or confront the classmate, it might be that God is placing these burdens in your heart to do something personally. "They" aren't going to do anything. "You" can at least try.

Let's imagine "Harry" comes to the group deeply troubled because his colleague at work is heading toward a divorce. As Harry asks the group to pray for his friend, the group begins to ask Harry how he's helping his friend. "Are you spending any additional time with your colleague?" one group member asks. "Have you told your friend that you'd like to pray for him?" asks another. Then the group begins to help Harry brainstorm ways he can minister to his co-worker that may preserve a marriage and draw the couple to Christ. On his own Harry might have cared, but might have been clueless that he could be part of the solution. I think this sort of thing happens all the time, and all we need is a group to remind us that there isn't a mysterious "they" out there ready to jump in. God is probably preparing "you" to be his hands and feet.

Keep Moving: Surviving the Roadblocks

I live in the rolling Kentucky countryside with my family (no jokes, please; we wear shoes, have our original teeth, don't make moonshine, and my wife is not my blood relation). In Kentucky they plotted roads by the way the cow wandered. Nothing is straight or flat. Each day I drive a beautiful stretch called Highway 22. One particular section of 22 is lovingly referred to by the locals as the "S-curve." As you might imagine, it is shaped like an "S." But the curve drops deeply into a small creek valley—limestone cliffs on one side and a guardrail protecting drivers from the gulch on the other—and then crosses a bridge and emerges. But for some reason, on rainy days people forget how to drive, the pavement gets a little slick, and someone ends up slammed into the guardrail or the limestone. I've never seen injured people, just banged-up cars. But inevitably on those accident days the police set up a roadblock and prevent travelers from using the S-curve. It's then I have a choice: wait at the roadblock for the wreck to clear or go several miles (and minutes) out of my way. I prefer to keep moving.

There are plenty of roadblocks that can stop us from serving and sharing. One group I was part of several years ago found that to be true. My small group decided we wanted to do a service project together, but we wanted it to be something personal and close to where we lived. That's when we stumbled on "Vietnam House." At least that's what I nicknamed the place because a jungle of shrubs, bushes, and trees overtook it. Karyn and I lived three doors down and had learned that the lady who owned the home was a recluse and had few resources to maintain the home. I convinced my group that it would be fun to surprise the lady by sprucing up her overrun place.

To be honest, my motives weren't exactly what you would call pure. Sure, I wanted to help an older lady in need. But I was so tired of looking at an overgrown forest in my neighbor's front yard. One cool, fall day the group descended on Vietnam House. We raked leaves, trimmed bushes, cut down a shrub the size of a VW Beetle, and removed small trees. We were proud of what our group accomplished in a short period of time. A couple of neighbors even stopped by and admired our work. Best of all, we did it all while the elderly neighbor was away. *Won't she be overjoyed when she sees the care we put into her home?* I innocently thought.

119

It was a few days later when I saw Edna and walked down the sidewalk to talk with her. Expecting a smile and a hug, I was stunned by her tongue-lashing! The VW Beetle shrub apparently doubled as the handrail on her porch steps. Now how was she supposed to get up the steps, she demanded of me. She then told me that the small trees provided "security" to keep people from peeking in her windows. According to her we had exposed her house to burglars. I was annoyed. We were cultivating missional lives, and she threw up a big roadblock! It would have been all too easy to say, "See, we tried to serve, and it turned out to be a waste of time."

Hey, sometimes serving goes awry! Sometimes we try to help people who never asked for our help, and they're not grateful. And sometimes we serve when asked and it still goes bad. It happens. A group volunteers together in the nursery and instead of thanks from parents picking up their infants, they are greeted by annoyed mothers and fathers that the check-in process took too long. A group of young people volunteers to paint an elderly man's house in the city, and as they work on his siding his able-bodied grandsons waltz out of the house and drive away in a new car. A group sacrifices a Tuesday evening to serve a meal at a shelter only to discover that the shelter has plenty of volunteers and they spend the evening standing around.

It's at those moments we should consider that success-fully cultivating missional lives does not require that the people we serve respond the way we want them to respond. When Jesus sent out his disciples to spread the Good News, he didn't tell the disciples they were successful only when people appreciated their message. No, he told them if people responded positively, stay with them and teach them, and if they didn't, move on (Matt. 10:1–15). Don't worry about the roadblocks, just keep moving.

Our small groups can help our members cultivate as we encourage each person to persevere. Let's return to our friend "Harry." Again, let's imagine he employs some of the advice his group offered. Let's pretend that he talks to his colleague from work. He offers to pray for him, tries to connect him with a Christian counselor, and offers to spend extra time with him. "Bug off!" his co-worker tells him. How should the group respond to Harry? Should they tell him he must have messed up? Should they tell him to try again? Or should they remind him that he did what he could and he shouldn't let this experience keep him from offering to help others? I think the latter choice is the best. It reminds him to keep moving even when he bumps into a roadblock.

Be Real: Avoiding the Veneer of Compassion

In recent years, missional living has become trendy. Thanks to guys like Bono, U2's front man, people who might not otherwise care much about what's happening in places like Africa suddenly show interest. A variety of businesses now offer "Project Red" products. If you buy special red iPods, computers, cell phones, and scarves, a portion of the profits go to help people with AIDS. No doubt, this is a good thing as it helps our world become more aware of a great tragedy. But it also provides a lovely opportunity to layer a thin veneer of compassion over an otherwise disinterested heart. Veneer is a thin coating of a quality wood, such as maple or mahogany, which spruces up a table made of wood particles and glue. A good veneer can cover a cheap piece of furniture.

If we were honest, the real reason many of us don't cultivate missional lives is that we simply don't want to be inconvenienced. However, we don't want anyone to know that we don't really care, so we cover it. We give the impression of compassion by asking for prayer requests for a friend, even if we're not helping that friend through their dilemma. We might even get involved in an overly simplistic way. A friend of mine used to wear a white rubber wristband imprinted with the word *one*. For a one-dollar investment he received the wristband, which was worn to communicate concern for people suffering from AIDS in Africa. After some time he quit wearing it. I asked why. Dan simply pointed out that a one-dollar investment and a rubber bracelet probably didn't go far enough to help the suffering. It almost trivialized suffering into a fashion statement. Of course, wearing a symbol to demonstrate concern isn't wrong, but if it's a veneer on an uninvolved heart, then it's just fake.

Our groups can help each member cultivate when we invite each participant to be real. As leaders we can create an environment of honesty where we are free to strip off the veneer. We can let our members confess that they don't care or don't know where to start. Imagine if your group members felt it was safe enough to admit that they didn't know what their spiritual gifts are, much less actually use them. Or confess that they are very private about their faith to neighbors and co-workers because they don't really know what to say without sounding "churchy." Encouraging (and modeling) that level of authenticity will move your group a point or two along the cultivating continuum, which I will talk about in the next chapter.

Sometimes our groups help us be real as we confess our particle board and glue compassion, and sometimes they challenge us. The longer a group is together, the more they tend to sense if someone is being real or layering on the veneer. Small group members should be able to ask each other, "Is that how you really feel?" And just as importantly they should ask, "What do you think you should do about it?" Group members can poignantly ask, "Do you really care?"

Ezekiel, a prophet thousands of years ago, wrote about broken, trampled, and wandering sheep in need of a good shepherd (Ezekiel 34). He described the sheep as wounded, scared, malnourished, and unhealthy. He chastised the leaders of Israel who did nothing to help the sheep they were charged with caring for. These bad shepherds looked good. They kept up the appearance of leadership, but underneath that veneer there was only self-centeredness. Ezekiel then described how a good shepherd would care for the flock. As a group, we can look at a passage like that as a window into the heart of God. If you are trying to help the members of your group be real, you can point them to Ezekiel 34 and ask them to assess which shepherd they most resemble.

Action First: Mission That Leads to Community

Every Easter my church produces a pageant. I know what you're thinking: big deal, a choir, a cheap set, and some kids dressed in bathrobes, right? Not quite. Three weeks of performances, attended by sixty-five thousand to eighty thousand people, who come to hear a timeless message performed at Broadway-level quality. Between the revolving platform and three-story set, it's pretty tremendous. And for those involved in the project it's pretty demanding. The cast and crew are there nearly every day for weeks leading up to the show, and then they are there every night for almost a month! A commitment like that can create some close ties, at least that's what some of the guys who played the Roman soldiers found out a few years ago.

These men suited up each night to rough up the man who played Christ. And while waiting for their time in the lights, they sat in the back huddled up. Tom, one of the men who played a soldier, said, "We had a lot of down time. So we used the time to pray for one another and for the people who were watching the show."

But once the performances came to an end, so did their relational connection. They discovered a huge gap. That's when an idea was forged. What if the guys who played the Roman soldiers formed a small group and studied Paul's letter to the Romans? Several guys jumped in. Tom was reluctant at first but caved in to the other guys. Tom went on to love it—which is good, since he now leads the group.

Eventually the group grew beyond the group of actors. Some of the soldiers' wives wanted in on this community. Then friends of the "soldiers" would find out about it and get invited in. As the years passed, the community has been tested. But according to Tom all those challenges have helped the group grow stronger.

For a number of people in that group, they would have never joined a group had the mission not come first. They were already deeply committed to cultivating missional lives, but they lacked a satisfying community. Serving became a doorway into a community that would also help them connect and change. The Roman soldiers group is not the only example of a community that emerged from service.

I think all serving teams should be concerned about connecting and changing. If a person attempts to serve or share their faith and a community does not back them, they run a great risk of their compassionate heart being squashed. For example, if a college student helps lead a children's small group each week but doesn't feel connected to others doing the same thing, her commitment to the mission will often slack. If an usher pushes bulletins week after week but doesn't know the ushers around him, he will often slip in his effort.

If your group is a serving team, you know what I mean. You probably weren't looking for a group, but because the mission sounded good you signed on. And then as you served alongside the same people regularly, you realized, "Hey, this is a group!" As you keep the task before you, you also enjoy helping each member connect with one another. If your team is doing well, you are probably aware that their health has a lot to do with the task (cultivating), the relationships (connecting), and the growth (change) they are experiencing.

Join Together

One of the great songs that show the synergistic way a group can work together to impact others was written more than thirty years ago by the poet Pete Townshend. OK, he wasn't poet as much as he was the songwriter for The Who, the famous British rock band of the 1960s and '70s. In the hit song "Join Together with the Band," Townshend implores everyone to jump in, regardless of appearance or skill.

The song begins with a folksy, twangy sound with just one instrument. But it builds in intensity as more instruments join in. What started as a dull, odd song ends as a powerful, moving piece. The song works because of the energizing way all the musicians work together.

All right, I'll admit we probably shouldn't put too much emphasis in a classic Who song to guide how we build missional communities. But the message is gripping. A band isn't a band if it's not making music. If people don't receive something from a group of musicians, then the band isn't doing what bands are supposed to do. What I love about the song is the message of acceptance. Regardless of where you are going, what you are wearing—even how well you play—this band wants you to join in and play. In fact, you can just hang out in the band and not play an instrument at all (presumably you'll help out in another way).

Imagine a community that firmly believed that each person needed to impact the world around him or her. The vigor derived from multiple instruments, all playing together, produced better music than any one instrument. The combined efforts would give the world better music and bless those who heard. We should abandon comfort and convenience for a truly great mission. Perhaps then we will enjoy the "biggest band you'll find," as Townshend worded it.

7

the nuts and bolts of cultivating

Helping People Become More Missional

Cultivating missional lives isn't just serving people in need. Nor is it just sharing your faith with those who don't know Jesus. It isn't simply supporting a missionary or using your spiritual gifts to grow other believers. It's all of these things and more. For most of human history, people assumed the sun revolved around the earth. About four hundred years ago scientists discovered the earth and its inhabitants revolved around the sun. We weren't the center of the universe! We're still getting used to not being the center. As we cultivate a missional life in our groups we will begin to remove the focus from ourselves and from our needs, and begin to look at the needs of those outside our groups. We will attempt to help our members develop compassionate hearts that beat for people who need the love of Jesus.

However, without intentional effort cultivating a missional life will remain a theory instead of a reality in many groups. People tend to be drawn to a group to build relationships or learn something they did not know. Fewer people join a group to learn to live missionally. But a group is a prime environment where we can explore spiritual gifts and calling, apply that understanding to a particular setting, and impact the world for Christ. It will help to explore the phases in which many groups work through when cultivating missional lives.

The Cultivating Continuum

The pattern of cultivating missional lives, like the other two patterns, has degrees of intensity. Depending on the goals of the group, success does not mean achieving a high intensity level of cultivating. As I have said with the continuums for connecting and changing, the goal is not to expect high concentration for all three patterns. It might be helpful to break the levels of cultivating down a bit. As a group helps each member begin to cultivate often, they learn about spiritual gifts and evangelism. Exploring is focused on learning as well as discovering places of ministry. If a group ratchets up the intensity a level to applying, they begin to encourage members to try out areas of service, engage friends in spiritual conversations, and perhaps occasionally serve together as a group. A group that begins to operate at a high-intensity level of cultivating is fully engaged in service—if not together as a group, then the group serves as a refueling station so individuals can minister outside of the group. This level is focused on sustainable impact on others. Let's explore each of those intensity phases in a bit more detail below.

Exploring

For most of us, cultivating missional lives begins by simply exploring our personality, passions, and spiritual gifts. In the low-intensity phase we may study spiritual gifts and evangelism, but most of the effort here is to help each member learn more than it is to get each member involved. Bible studies and discussions are primary pathways for groups to help each other explore how God has wired them to help others. Group members who are exploring learn that each one of us is intended to be the hands and feet of Christ. During this point along the continuum group members are challenged to think about how God might help them minister to others at work, school, or neighborhood.

I'd like you to meet Terri and Heather, sisters who have attended church their whole lives. Even though they grew up in children's church, then youth group, and even Christian camp in the summer, they were pretty naïve about the whole idea of serving and evangelism when they showed up to their small group for college-aged students. The leader of the group thought it would be a good idea to study spiritual gifts. Terri and Heather joined the group to hang out with other students and didn't really care what they discussed. But within a few weeks they were curious. They learned that every Christian has a spiritual gift and using those gifts helps make everyone spiritually stronger.

Applying

During the medium-intensity level of cultivating, the focus shifts from head knowledge to heart response. Groups in this phase challenge each person to use their gifts and begin to serve others outside of the Christian community. This often involves a lot of exploration, since finding just the right place to serve takes trial and error for many of us. A group member might know they have a teaching gift, but during this phase they start out teaching fourth graders only to discover they don't have patience for that age group. Next they try teaching high school sophomores before they finally realize that teaching college students is the best place for them. Applying is a very active phase. Group members are just trying to seek the place where God has called them.

Let's check in again with Heather and Terri. As the group of college students dialogued more about spiritual gifts, the sisters decided to take a test that would help them figure out their gifts. After replying to 150 questions, they scored their test and shared the results with the group. Heather's test revealed that she had the gift of teaching, while Terri had a strong administrative gift. Unsure where to plug in, both young women asked a few different ministries within their church if they could "try out" those ministries. At first Terri helped in the church office a couple of hours for a few weeks. She liked it but felt it was "busy work." Then she asked the children's ministry director if she could try organizing upcoming lesson plans for the various age levels. She found that very satisfying. Her sister, Heather, likewise tried out a couple of different ministries before finding the right fit. She tried teaching sixth grade girls but just couldn't connect. When she tried again with first grade girls, she had a blast.

Impacting

For groups cultivating at a high intensity level, the goal is often to maximize impact. Members find they have an inner confidence that they are serving precisely where God would have them. Sometimes this is referred to as finding our "calling." When an impacting person is serving in their "sweet spot" they are energized. Markus Buckingham, author of *Now Discover Your Strengths*, says that when we are operating in our strengths we feel "magnificent." It sounds funny, doesn't it? But when we find the right overlap of our gifts and a place of need, we feel great, don't we? When we are impacting, we might get worn emotionally, but we are energized.

It took Terri and Heather just over six months, but they found opportunities to use their gifts to help others and at the same time felt energized by the experience. Terri soon became the "right hand" person for the children's ministry director. Her skills of administration played out in how she coordinated upcoming curriculum—she even helped lead a team that organized the ministry storage closet. Meanwhile, Heather became more than a teacher to her first grade girls. She made special birthday cards for them, took them for extra adventures every few months, and was thrilled when the girls initiated spiritual conversations.

Where Is Your Group?

Before you employ the nuts and bolts of connecting, it's helpful to identify which phase of connecting most of your group is in. Think through these questions:

- Does each person in your group understand and know their spiritual gifts?
- Do they understand that we are the hands and feet of Jesus and he has a unique assignment for each one of us?
- Has the group discussed the unique context of ministry in which God has placed each of us?

If you answered no to most of these, your group is likely cultivating at the exploring phase.

- Has your group served together?
- Do group members discuss areas of ministry that they have tried out?
- Has at least half of the group found an area of ministry to which they are committed?

If you answered no to most of these, your group is likely cultivating at the applying phase.

- Do your members regularly serve (together or separately)?
- Do group members discuss how they are helping others?
- Does participating in ministry energize the group?

If you answered yes to most of these, your group is likely cultivating at the impacting phase.

What Can Help Group Members Cultivate during the Exploring Phase?

Discuss Spiritual Gifts

The next time your group is choosing a Bible study, you may want to pick one that is focused on spiritual gifts. Many people who have attended church for years are unaware that God has given them a spiritual gift. They may have heard about spiritual gifts but are pretty clueless that everyone who has a relationship with Jesus has a gift, including them. Helping your members explore their spiritual gifts is one of the easiest things you can do to begin helping them cultivate missional lives.

I grew up in a Baptist church. Whenever the lights were on, my parents dragged me to church. Sunday school, worship service, Wednesday prayer meeting, the occasional potluck—you name it, I was there. Even if my heart wasn't there, my body was at Awana (a children's program), then to youth group. In my late teen years my parents' praying paid off, and I began to desire to grow closer to Christ without their strong-arming me. About that time I began to wonder if I could or should become a pastor. I wasn't exactly sure if it was something you signed up for or if an angel magically appeared and told you that you had no choice. I remember asking the pastor of our small church what he thought. "If you can do anything else, do it!" he quickly replied. I figured

132

either he really hated his job or he figured it was a high calling that should be entered into soberly (I'm hoping it was the latter). But along the way he suggested I take a test to see if I had the "right" spiritual gifts. I knew how to take tests, so on a summer afternoon in the fireside room at our church I filled out a questionnaire.

I recall anxiously anticipating the results. Would I pass? What if I failed? What then? Days later as I sat across from him in his small study, surrounded by books, he told me the good news. I passed and probably had the right "gift mix" for the job! I was sort of relieved and sort of confused. I really didn't know what he was talking about. That was my first run-in with the idea that God gives people gifts. It didn't really occur to me at the time that *everyone* who follows Christ has a gift! Of course *I* did; I was going to be a pastor. I mean, pastors have a spiritual gift; that's how they get the job, right? *The average church attender doesn't have a gift, do they?* I wondered.

It was years later and a theology degree under my belt before I understood that the Holy Spirit has given every Christian special gifts in order to help build the Body of Christ (Ephesians 4). I can't help but wonder, if it took me that long to lock in the idea and really begin to accept my gifts, what about the school teacher or truck driver who don't necessarily spend as much time reading about theology. Maybe as you read this you're saying, boy, what are my spiritual gifts? Like with me all those years ago, the whole topic might be downright confusing. That's just fine. Take several group meetings and study spiritual gifts. There are plenty of curricula from which to choose and more come out every year.[1]

Discuss Evangelism

We can also focus our group members on learning to share their faith. Let's be honest—evangelism is probably the most intimidating subject for a group to tackle. What if we start to share our faith with a neighbor and they turn out to be a championship debater for the Atheist society? Or what if we invite a friend at work to church and they turn out to be a very argumentative Scientologist? We probably imagine more scary scenarios than we will ever bump into. However, as a group you can remove some pressure by simply working through a Bible study that takes a close look at the gospel. Some Bible studies focus on helping people have spiritual conversations with others and some of them just focus on how Jesus interacted with lost people. Just discussing the importance of loving lost people helps cultivate.

Shortly after I joined the staff of my old church, the leadership decided we should help our people become more evangelistic. We grabbed a popular series on evangelism and all but begged our small groups to go through it. Many agreed to use the materials we supplied them. I remember visiting Gary's group of young single men one evening. They were a mix of skilled craftsmen and working professionals all beginning their careers. As I sat in the apartment filled with a hodgepodge of your typical young bachelor furniture, Gary began the discussion. As I recall they spent most of their time discussing what was wrong with the curriculum. The questions weren't helpful, the suggestions were lame, and they weren't sure that the material would actually work. At first it seemed like the discussion was veering way off course. Then I realized that this is how a bunch of young guys often discuss anything. From sports to politics or work, it's more like a group of pundits evaluating the subject than a group of scholars digesting concepts. I came away realizing that they were learning quite a bit about how to have spiritual conversations with people, albeit not the way the author probably hoped they would!

The point of a discussion on evangelism isn't to find a "silver bullet" that makes witnessing a snap or boils the gospel down to a twenty-second cliché. No, I think evangelism discussions help nudge us toward open hearts for lost people. It reminds us to care and to engage our friends who are outside of faith in good conversation.

Investigate Where God Is Working

Nearly twenty years ago, authors Henry Blackaby and Claude King reminded believers that God is always working around us. In their book *Experiencing God* they pointed to a teaching by Jesus where he clearly communicates that the Son could do nothing on his own; instead, he looked to see where the Father was already working and joined him there (John 5:17–20). They challenged readers to live like Jesus and look around for evidence of God's work and join him. They suggested that we listen to classmates and co-workers for spiritual interest or personal struggles and try to point them to Christ. It took a lot of pressure off of abruptly bringing up God to unsuspecting colleagues.

When Jeremy talked to our men's group about his life direction, he couldn't get one burning idea out of his head: Bolivia. A friend of his oversaw a mission in the South American country and desperately needed an airplane mechanic for a short stint while another missionary was on furlough. And guess what, Jeremy was just such a mechanic. As a single guy who rented a house, he didn't have a lot of commitments holding him down. Over the weeks and month our group prayed with him about how God might be working in his life, and after serious soul searching he took the plunge. Jeremy didn't come up with a plan and ask God to get on board with it; he simply asked the group to help him investigate where God was already working and how Jeremy could be part of that. For over a year Jeremy kept a much-needed fleet of planes flying over the jungles of Bolivia.

135

What Can Help Group Members Cultivate during the Applying Phase?

Serve Together a Few Times a Year

One great thing groups can do together to cultivate missional lives is to serve together. This can be as simple as offering to clean an area of the church after the worship service or something far more involved. Small group leaders Chris and Pat figured out a way to build their community while they accomplished a very important (and somewhat tedious) task. As head usher, Chris had the duty to prepare the communion trays for communion Sundays. When the church was small, it took a couple of people less than an hour, but as the church grew by thousands it was more than two people could handle. One Saturday evening I was passing through the church kitchen when I bumped into a cheerful group of chatty people. At first it looked more like a party than a work crew. There was laughter and smiles and lots of activity. Then I noticed that everyone was wearing plastic gloves. *Odd attire for a social event,* I thought. Some people were sorting small plastic cups into the communion cup trays while others filled the cups with juice. Other folks were placing small cracker pieces into the bread trays. It took me a few minutes to realize that this wasn't just a crew of random volunteers; this was Chris and Pat's group! As it turned out, the group worked together each time communion was to be served. They spent some time together focusing on others.

Adopt a Missionary

Perhaps your group isn't quite ready to jump into an area of service together. If your members complain about the time it would take to serve together or how they can't make another commitment, you could suggest that your group adopt a missionary or ministry. Think of this as low-impact aerobics. You still have the opportunity to help your group focus on the needs of others without ever leaving the cozy confines of the family room.

A few years ago while on a trip in Kenya and Tanzania, I had a startling conversation with a missionary. Fred was an American missionary who had been in Tanzania for well over twenty years by the time I met him. Fred seemed far more at home in Mwanza, a large city on the shore of Lake Victoria, than I could ever imagine him in an American city like Chicago or Atlanta. As I recall, he even wore a safari-styled shirt. I was in East Africa with three others from the church I worked for at the time to look for ministries to partner with. As I talked with Fred, I was saddened by how abandoned he felt by his home church. "I don't think anyone knows what I do over here or even cares," Fred told me. We were sharing a paper basket of deep fried "mystery meat" as we talked. "I'm thankful for the churches that support me, but I feel very disconnected from them." There was a painful longing in his voice. Obviously his supporting churches cared about him and the work he did, otherwise they probably wouldn't fund his ministry, but he wished for some relational connection as well. It struck me then that a small group working on cultivating could be of tremendous help to people like Fred. Imagine if a small group from Fred's church emailed him regularly. They could link arms with Fred in prayer, even though they were thousands of miles apart. As a result, the group would learn about the physical and spiritual needs of another culture. That group would gain a global perspective and would really begin to live out a missional perspective.

Adopt a Ministry

Your group doesn't have to only look to global missions if you're trying to cultivate missional lives. You may want to adopt a ministry much closer to home. Your group could become prayer partners with one of the ministries within your own church. Imagine the thrill of the youth pastor if you call him up and tell him that your group would like to regularly pray for the student ministry. You could ask him to email you specific requests for prayer. Perhaps you could push this a step further and offer to bring the youth volunteers dinner one night before the youth group meets. Just like adopting a missionary, adopting a ministry can start out by simply praying for specific needs and eventually morph into something more involved. It's up to you and your group.

What Can Help Group Members Cultivate during the Impacting Phase?

Acts of Regular Kindness (ARK)

I have to admit, I'm not a huge fan of the term "Random Act of Kindness."[2] While it's nice to show random acts of kindness—like returning a shopping cart for a young mom who is wrestling her kids into the minivan—it also seems to give us permission that we are off the hook from regularly helping. Let's face it: random is easier than regular. By helping out at the occasional service project, we placate our conscience enough that we become convinced we've done enough. Rather than pursue a lifestyle of kindness and helping, random acts of kindness become more like a holiday that comes once every blue moon. Instead, I encourage groups to pursue Acts of Regular Kindness (ARK). The distinction is that ARK is frequent and purposeful. In this kind of ARK we plan how we can serve others. We see where there is need and we commit to helping.

Several years ago my wife and I became good friends with our neighbors Albert and Lana. I think we may have been the only people in America who actually took a fence down between properties so that we could better connect with our neighbors. The four of us had a few things in common. We were young, starting our families, and early in our careers. But Lana and Albert had us beat in the kid department. We had two and they had four—and she was pregnant! Did I mention all of her kids were under the age of five at the time?

What complicated matters for them was that their family was thousands of miles away, in the Middle East. There was no doubt they needed good friends as they waited for the baby to come, and we were looking forward to being extra hands. Our plans to help were severely altered one January afternoon when my wife, Karyn, was nearly crippled in a car accident. Over the following months of her physical recovery we could barely take care of our own children and ourselves, much less help anyone else. That's when my brilliant wife approached a small group of women to adopt Lana. It wasn't a hard sell.

It just so happened that this group of single women was a mix of social workers and experts on early childhood development. They latched on to the mission with gusto. The women developed friendships with the young mother, and she was thrilled to receive some new friends. Before too long they began visiting her and the children frequently. In fact, the women invited a small group of single men to join in their services as well. Albert was an extremely hard worker with two jobs, so it was difficult to keep up on all the household chores. The two small groups coordinated a "spring cleanup day" and in a few hours worked wonders and had a lot of fun! A couple of the guys really bonded with the oldest son and would return with the women to play soccer or video games with him. Those groups became part of the family—invited to birthdays and holiday celebrations. When the fifth baby joined the family, the chaos was abated by the regular presence of these caring young women.

The opportunity to serve this family wasn't an obligation; it was an opportunity. As they focused on Lana and her children, they demonstrated Christ's love for people in need. They adopted the family and in return they were adopted into that family.

You may wonder how this is different from groups that serve together during the applying phase. The main distinction is how frequent your group serves together and how intense the involvement of each group member is to the task. Chris and Pat's group served together several times a year when the church prepared communion. The group that served Lana and Albert sometimes served several times within a two-week period. A group that serves together might give a few hours once a month or less, while a group that is ARK-focused might give a few hours each week. Both are great ways for your group to cultivate missional lives. Determining the level of involvement that is right for your group really depends on what level of commitment your group wants to give.

Become a Serving Team

Some groups redefine their purpose as they grow together. That happened to my friend Jamie's group. Her group of couples from southern Indiana developed a remarkable kinship with each other. As Jamie's group journeyed together they built relationships and challenged each other to grow. But along the way they began to ask each other what God would have them do next. They valued their community and did not want to lose what they were enjoying. But they also knew that if they didn't come up with another purpose for their gathering, their group would probably run out of steam.

One evening in the early summer I drove across the Ohio River with my friend Susan and her husband Lance to talk about an interesting proposal with Jamie's group. Over Chinese takeout spread across the biggest table I think I'd ever seen, we asked these veteran group members for help. Would they be willing to help us form new small groups and then provide guidance to the new leaders? After all, they were experienced group members and had a pretty good picture of what a healthy group should look like. I expected most people to say, "We'll get back to you." But instead I was greeted with enthusiasm. They were ready to sign up! Jamie's group now acts more like a serving team as they have adopted an outward focus and coach leaders and partner with the staff team in forming new small groups.

Becoming a serving team is certainly not for every group. But if the majority of your members feel a tug toward the same area of ministry, it is a great option. It can also breathe new life in a group that is well connected and tired of just spending their time in discussion.

Support Each Other in Individual Ministries

Perhaps your group doesn't serve together but most of the members of your group are regularly engaged in a meaningful ministry. When they meet, they swap stories of God's work around them. Each person is impacting others and they retreat to the group for mutual encouragement and prayer.

The longer my group with Doug and Josh met, the more we developed the missional pattern of cultivating. All three of us served as elders at our church, but we were also involved in other missional endeavors. Doug oversaw our first video venue (a church within the larger church with live music but a video feed from the main auditorium), Josh was a small group leader for first grade boys, and I was working with our small groups team on the church staff. Besides that, Doug owned his own business and Josh was a salesman, and they often talked of how they attempted to serve others in their corporate world. We always spent some time discussing the challenges of serving others and living for Christ in our individual ministries. We offered advice when asked, but mostly we listened, encouraged each other, and prayed for each other. The group became an important refueling station as we served others.

At one particular meeting Josh described an interaction with Al, a client with whom he worked in southern Michigan. Josh described to our group how his conversation with Al swung from the product he was trying to sell and turned to spiritual things. Al's openness surprised Josh. As he poured out his problems—the bad decisions he had made and the repercussions from those decisions—Josh listened. As Josh told Al about the importance of a connection with God and with a good church, Al listened. When Josh told our group, he asked us to pray for Al, which we did. But we prayed for Josh too, that he would continue to be a presence for God in his work. As our group did this, we were nurturing the missional pattern of cultivating.

Reflection

Before moving on, take a few moments and reflect on these questions.

1. Read Ezekiel 34. What are the characteristics of the bad shepherds? What are the characteristics of the good shepherd?

2. Why is cultivating missional lives so important for your group?

3. How has your group helped your members discover their spiritual gifts and their place of serving?

4. In what phase of cultivating (exploring, applying, impacting) is your group?

5. Which idea from the nuts and bolts chapter would you like to try in your group?

6. What are other ways you can help your members develop missional lives?

part 4

harmony

Pulling It All Together

har * mo * ny [hahr-muh-nee]

Creating a pleasing combination of the three
patterns that leads to a strong community.

8

when good groups go bad

The Pitfall of Obsession

I have a secret. I love interior design. All right, I'll be the first to admit, it's not very manly. Men are supposed to prefer *Sports Illustrated* and ESPN, but I don't. I read my wife's *Martha Stewart Living* magazine (sometimes before she does). At least my subscription to *This Old House* magazine isn't as questionable. Perhaps I shouldn't mention that I asked my parents for a subscription to *Metropolitan Home* magazine back in high school—I guess there are worse things for a high school boy to read. All this to say, I know way more than the average man about interior design and home furnishings.

One of the great principles when it comes to decorating a living space is harmony. You can have an antique in a modern downtown flat if it harmonizes with the other pieces. You can use Grandma's old steamer trunk as a coffee table in the family room if it lives in harmony with the corduroy sofa. In fact, companies like Pottery Barn prove that you can mix old and new styles and still have a fresh-looking space. It's not about balancing different styles. You don't have to have an equal number of antiques to new pieces for it to work. You don't need two oak end tables to balance out the maple coffee table and credenza (am I scaring you yet?).

Have you ever walked into a house and thought, *Hmm, I think they really like country kitsch*? Every room is chock-full of plaids, and doilies cover every table. Big baskets hold little baskets, which hold still smaller baskets. Each room looks like the Cracker Barrel lobby blew up inside their house. Okay, if this sort of describes your home, let me apologize right now. I still respect you and think you're great. But that sort of obsession overpowers a room, wouldn't you agree? Ultimately a living space should make us glad we're in it, but a room that is overpowered by one obsession can overwhelm the senses and make us uncomfortable.

All right, I'll get to my point. When it comes to a great small group, you don't have to try to balance out the patterns of connecting, changing, and cultivating. Instead, you should try to harmonize them. Try to include relationship building while you help people change and also keep an outward focus. You don't have to develop each pattern with equal intensity. But as you try to harmonize the patterns, also try to avoid letting one pattern become the obsession of your group and swamp all the others. The Cracker Barrel is great, just not in excess!

bal * ance [bal-uhns] *verb*—a state of equilibrium; equal distribution of time, effort, energy, etc.

har * mo * ny [hahr-muh-nee] *noun*—a simultaneous combination of connecting, changing, and cultivating that produces a helpful effect.

The Pitfall of Pattern-Obsession

As you explored the three patterns, no doubt one of them resonated more than the others with you. Perhaps as you read about connecting it made you smile and you thought, *Yes, this is my group! This is where we are at!* As you read the nuts and bolts chapter you began to make notes of how you would accelerate that favored pattern in your group. And as you read one or two of the other patterns, you thought, *This isn't that interesting. I'll just focus on the pattern we're best at and forget the other two.* Ignoring the other two patterns may work for a while, but let me caution you about what I affectionately refer to as "pattern obsession." That's when a group gets so preoccupied with one pattern that they neglect the other two. It might help if I broke down how each pattern obsession can create problems.

Connecting-Obsessed Group

A group that is obsessed with connecting might start strong but end with a fizzle. My friend Nick stood on the precipice of a dying group. Over café Americanos at Starbucks, Nick poured out his struggle. "Our group was going great. All three guys faithfully showed up week after week. We were really tight! And then one by one guys started missing. Then the excuses came, and now all three say they don't have time for it anymore. What went wrong?" I asked Nick to describe how often they met, where they met, and what they did during their meeting.

"We met at 6:30 every Thursday at the Waffle House for an hour or so."

"So what did you *do*?" I again asked him.

"We talked."

At this point I must have developed a puzzled look because Nick then filled in the gap. "We talked about sports, politics, family, work. Really whatever the guys had on their minds."

149

I began to get the picture. Nick meant well. He thought, *Hey, I'll get some guys together and we'll have community.* What he didn't realize was that the connecting pattern alone would not hold a group together for long. Most groups need something more than that. They need another purpose, such as changing or cultivating. Unless the group became best of friends, a weekly commitment for mild friends isn't worth the effort. As I coached Nick, I suggested that he include something that would help the guys change to become more like Christ. I talked with him about how the group could help each guy be a better witness for Christ at work and home. If the guys saw their group also as a spiritual refueling station that gave them the energy to keep moving closer to Christ, it might revive the dying group.

You can't blame Nick for becoming connecting-obsessive. Many people scramble to find meaningful relationships. They long to develop deep connections, especially in a world wrought with divorce, overstretched lives, and fractured relationships. The desire for friendship is good. But most groups will buckle under the pressure of a connecting-obsessed group without the change and cultivate patterns. Without harmony, the experience will likely end up just like Nick's.

Change-Obsessed Group

Change-obsessed groups are easy to spot. Usually they have an insatiable thirst for intense "Bible study."[1] They will meet for a couple of hours and keep side conversations to a bare minimum as they do the "important work" of deep study. I have to admit, it seems wrong to say anything bad about this obsession. How could I criticize a group of people who are deeply obsessed with changing? Through the years I have helped launch more than fifty groups that were concerned only with change. Actually, they were concerned with money—how to better handle it and how to become more like Christ in the process. We started hundreds of people in an excellent ten-week curriculum focused on Christian perspectives on finances. However, over the years of using this curriculum only a few groups continued on after the material ended. It didn't matter how we formed the groups, how we coached the leaders, or how we prepared the participants. Immediately after the ten-week period, over 90 percent of the groups fell apart. Even though the participants did homework each week, memorized Scripture, and even took turns leading the discussion, nearly all of the groups ended on their tenth week! It doesn't seem possible, does it? I wouldn't believe it either if I weren't a witness.

For years my former church has used great study material to help individuals become more like Christ in the area of financial stewardship; in other words, the groups were focused on change (pardon the pun). I'll admit, the material is helpful and many people have come away better financial stewards and on a path to financial freedom. However, the material has one glaring flaw: it crushes small groups. I think I may know why.

When Karyn and I joined one of these financial stewardship groups several years ago, we were excited. Actually, Karyn was the excited one, hoping that it would help me since I'm ridiculous with money. I'm slightly dyslexic when it comes to numbers (at least that's my self-diagnosed excuse), so financial common sense has never been my strong suit. Without my wise wife I'd be in a very bad spot financially. As the group began, I was looking forward to learning some new skills. I was also looking forward to getting to know some new people. We were already friends with Mike and Karen as well as Rob and Amy, who were all younger couples like we were, but we met with five new people as well. Lec and Anna, a couple in their early grandparent years, helped balance out the six of us, who were all beginning the baby years. Jeff, a single salesman, was new to town and added some more interest. There was one other couple, with junior high age sons, who rounded us out.

151

The material was highly structured. We had two hours to meet, which included pages of questions that must be answered and a short video promoting other products available through the ministry. Side conversations had to be kept to a minimum; discussion was discouraged, since the limited time available was to be spent affirming the answers to the questions in the book. The closest thing to relational development was the one potluck scheduled halfway through and a brief time to share prayer requests at the end of each session.

I've painted a fairly negative picture of this curriculum, which is not my intent. It does a pretty good job of helping people change, but that alone won't keep most groups together. While these financial stewardship groups were change obsessed, they neglected connecting and cultivating. That obsession ultimately squashed the little community that was beginning to form. Imagine the power of change that could have taken place if the groups stayed together. Our group could have moved on to another subject, but in the backdrop we could always return to the topic of finances. In the long run change might have been even more significant as we journeyed with some of the same people beyond ten weeks. Perhaps we would have been less likely to return to old ways of doing things and the change would have been permanent.

Cultivating-Obsessed Group

Groups that become obsessed with the cultivating pattern are an interesting phenomenon. They are so preoccupied with a ministry or a task that they leave little time to nurture relationships with each other or help each other grow spiritually. Nearly every church has a bunch of cultivate-obsessed groups, although they rarely think of them as groups—which is part of the problem. When a couple of dozen people volunteer to help with third and fourth graders each week, they are a serving group, whether they see that or not. When four couples work in the nursery every other Sunday morning, they are a serving group. And when a handful of men pass out bulletins week after week, they are a serving group, even if that's not how they see it. These groups have active participants who are committed to cultivating missional lives as they serve. However, for many of these participants, if they don't form some good relationships and become better followers of Christ along the way, their commitment will likely run out. My friend Jenny was in a group like that.

A few years ago she formed a team with a mission: coordinate a Christmas project for our church. In mid-September she gathered seven other people together to plan and prepare for the thousands of donated gifts that would hopefully come in that year for children in need. The group worked tightly together, anticipating all the details for a successful project. "We met often," Jenny said. "We even ate together a couple of times a month leading up to the time we collected the items." But as soon as the project was over, so was the group. "I still say hi when I see the people I worked with," she said with a level of disappointment. They nailed the pattern of cultivating, but if they wanted the group to go on after the project, they needed to spend time connecting and changing. Sure, some cultivate-obsessed groups are designed to last only for a short season, but in my experience many people lament forming some relationships and then "poof" the group is gone, unlike the Roman soldier group, which wove in connecting and cultivating and still enjoys meeting.

Pattern Mania

I am not suggesting that a solution to this mania is to become obsessed with all three patterns. Your group will also be crushed if you try to drive all three patterns with equal ferocity. Instead, what we need is harmony of the three patterns, which I will talk about next.

9

real simple

Harmony of the Three C's

Harmony of connecting, changing, and cultivating is the key to a simple small group. When the three patterns work together, a group will achieve synergy. The energy derived from a community that builds relationships, helps members become like Jesus, and lives missionally will be greater than the energy produced by focusing on only one of the three. But harmony is prized more than balance.

A group that does not give equal portions of energy and time to each of the three patterns is not a failure. It is not flawed. If simple small groups required balancing the three C's, every group leader would feel like a failure. In fact, I believe that when most people use the term "balance," they really mean harmony. Years ago when I worked in college student development, my boss would tell her staff that we should make sure we lived balanced lives. We should get rest, private time, exercise, and work hard. Since her staff not only worked on campus but also lived in the residence halls with students, balance wasn't remotely possible. Besides, she worked far more than forty or fifty hours a week. After we pushed her, she agreed that balance was a nice goal but not something we could live out all the time. I do think she was right; however, she just used the wrong word. We could have a harmonious life. We needed sleep and a healthy lifestyle and we needed to work hard. But some weeks we needed to put in sixty-five hours of work and others thirty-five. We needed sleep, but when a crisis erupted at 2:00 a.m., balance went out the window. Harmony is how we deal with the nonnegotiable pieces of our life in a way that keeps us from imploding.[1] It's what helps our group become energized and keeps it healthy.

I love Christmastime and every year try to convince my wife to let me put up the Christmas decorations earlier and earlier. (When she says no, I say it just reflects that she doesn't love Jesus as much as I do!) When Karyn and I were first married and at Calvin College, we would attend the annual performance of Handel's *Messiah*. Now, I don't know much about music, but I know that the word *harmony* is generally used as a musical term. Imagine if George Frideric Handel had to balance the music. The violin had to play the exact number of notes as the oboe, the harpsichord the same number as the tuba. The Hallelujah Chorus wouldn't be nearly as amazing! In fact, I think that striving for balance would turn majestically beautiful music into cacophonous noise. Similarly, the *Messiah* performed with just the violin, or just the oboe, or just the timpani would not have survived since 1741 as one of the world's greatest musical compositions.

Synergy of the Three Patterns

Instead of balance (or pattern-obsession), a group can strive for harmony of connecting, changing, and cultivating. The outcome of the different patterns working together produces a synergy that produces far more than any individual pattern could. The upshot of such a community, as Luke writes, is that the community is seen as favorable to the people around them, "enjoying the favor of all the people. And the Lord added to their number daily those who were being saved" (Acts 2:47). In his commentary on the passage Darrell Bock writes,

> The finding favor is noted only here in Acts. This combination of terms . . . appears in a few New Testament texts. . . . The idea is that others are appreciative of this new community. A vibrant community extends itself in two directions: toward God and toward neighbor. A veiled reference to the great commandment appears here.
>
> In sum, Luke affirms the internal fellowship, intimacy, and engagement of the community. This positive activity is accompanied by joy and glad hearts, and their worship and praise of God are ongoing. But this is not an isolated, private club or hermetically sealed community. Their reputation with outsiders also is good.[2]

Bock points out the obvious, that the church, in its earliest state, was magnetic because people cared for their own, were growing in Christlikeness, and were impacting the world around them. This is the synergy that our groups still have the potential to live out. It was not meant as a footnote to history but an inspirational snapshot of what a Christ-focused community is capable of.

The Connecting-Focused Group

If we want to maintain a harmony of the three C's we should focus on one pattern and include the other two. For instance, when a group is new I encourage them to focus most of their energy on the connecting pattern. They should spend extra time getting to know each other and socializing. Build the relational bridge strong. We live in a community-starved world; celebrating a group that begins to belong to one another is a great thing. But a group that is focused should also consider how to include the other patterns.

Such a group might still spend the majority of their meeting time discussing a section from the Bible. But they focus less on a study and more on a discussion in which everyone participates. They may even pick a discussion guide that has fewer questions, giving them more time to "rabbit trail" the discussion. They still include the change pattern as they discuss the Scriptures and apply them to life; they just do it in a very relational way. And they include cultivating in their group by discussing how God is teaching them to help others at work, school, and in their neighborhood. From time to time they may even serve together. But the undeniable focus of the group is connecting with one another.

The Change-Focused Group

The group focused on helping each member change devotes the majority of their energy to becoming more like Christ. Perhaps each member joined the group to become doctrinally stable. They wanted to know what to believe and why it's important. Maybe they grew tired of saying, "I believe because I feel it in my heart," and they wanted to be better rooted in their faith. Some groups that are change-focused are dedicated to behavioral change. A man who is tired of his addictive behaviors and wants to change or a woman who is worn out by her angry demeanor and wants to become more peaceful are looking to change behaviors, and they turn to a group to help them change.

A group focused on change might spend more time holding up the mirror for each other and lovingly carefronting one another. They might partner with each other to memorize Scripture. Maybe the group becomes more classroom-based and brings in a gifted teacher or chooses a DVD series. As they help each other change they also continue to build relationships, understanding that they can help each other more if there is relational trust. Perhaps they arrange special social times that don't interfere with their learning time but leave room for connecting. They cultivate by encouraging one another to live out their unique calling and serve where God has placed them.

The Cultivating-Focused Group

The group focused on helping each member cultivate a missional life is often a task-based small group or serving team. They are usually preoccupied with helping others—particularly those who need spiritual help—grow closer to Christ. However, sometimes these groups have a mission that serves the church, such as working together to shepherd third graders. They might be a gathering of small group coaches who connect with each other around the care of leaders. Perhaps it's a group that conducts a worship service and small groups twice a month at the local penitentiary. The members of the group may be engaged in a ministry together or they may be serving individually, but they use the group to refresh and recharge one another.

A group focused on cultivating might spend all their time shoulder-to-shoulder ministering to others, but they don't forget to connect and change. What defines them as a group may be their service, but what keeps them coming back might be the relationships they forge with one another. Before they serve, they have a quick huddle and give the one-minute update of what's happening in their lives. They may communicate outside of the mission through email or phone calls. Perhaps the change pattern is instigated by one person in the group taking on a chaplain-like role and encouraging each person in his or her faith. Or they set aside a brief devotional time and read and apply a few passages of Scripture.

What If a Pattern Is Missing?

Shortly after moving to a new state, my friend Tim joined a group that was primarily focused, maybe even obsessed, with change. The group gathered, watched a video, and then discussed it. With twenty people, it was a very large small group. Tim quickly realized the group was made up of two or three clusters of friends (I think the less polite word is *cliques*). Since he wasn't part of any of those clusters, he was usually ignored. Tim told me that when he arrived at the host's home he would stand near the refreshments and smile at the people filling their plates, hoping to make a friend or two. "They actually didn't even look at me! Can you believe it?" Tim asked incredulously. To be honest, Tim told me, some people did greet him, but they were always looking over his shoulder for their "real" friends to come through the door—and when they did, Tim got ditched. Finally, the host would just call everyone to the family room and turn on the TV. For the next thirty minutes the group would stare at the TV. Sometimes they would stay together as a group for some follow-up questions and sometimes they would break into smaller groups—though never the same groups. That wasn't much better, Tim described to me. "It was like being the last picked for kickball at recess in elementary school."

Perhaps the most noticeable sign that the group wasn't connecting was indicated by the prayer time. Tim explained to me that most of the requests seemed fake. The group attenders shared requests for long-lost relatives or neighbors they didn't really know, and one even requested prayer for the relative of a co-worker whose name she had forgotten! But the prayers indicated nothing personal. Since no one seemed comfortable sharing anything personal, Tim withheld too.

The problem seemed pretty obvious to me: the group completely ignored the relational pattern. Maybe they assumed enough people knew each other that the rest would eventually catch on. But as a result, Tim told me, he never felt comfortable. Since he's relatively shy, he didn't feel comfortable pushing himself on the other people in the group. Extroverts like me can jump into a room of strangers and make friends relatively quickly. But roughly half the population is

160

like Tim, and would connect better if a group was sensitive to the connecting pattern.

Without a growing relational connection it was easy for Tim to miss group meetings. If something came up at work or a friend needed help, he skipped the group without much anxiety. The cultivating pattern was absent as well. Tim realized that some in the group were engaged in areas of service, but as a theme within the group it was hit or miss. He was more likely to hear one of the guys talk about the merits of a 1080 dpi LCD TV than he was to hear about a friend at work someone was ministering to. There was no mention of serving, no exploration of spiritual gifts, and no encouragement to reach out to friends. Eventually, feeling isolated in a small group wore Tim out, and he threw in the towel. I can't blame him for giving up, but it grieved me since this problem is easy to solve.

I wish Tim's story was unique, but it's far too common. Many groups become pattern-obsessed rather than pursue the tension of pattern harmony. I wonder if Tim's group would have established the relationships first how much stronger it would be. If they connected with each other, perhaps they would have established the trust that would have encouraged them to be open. Perhaps my friend Tim, a keenly insightful guy with a background in missions, would have contributed more to the discussion. And perhaps he would have helped others grow. As Alan Deutschman pointed out in his book *Change or Die*, people are most likely to change in relationships. Connecting is vitally important if we expect people to change to be more like Christ. If a group like Tim's simply included some relational and missional elements into their group, the connecting and cultivating patterns would emerge.

- Spend twenty minutes of group time with an icebreaker that includes everyone.
- Insist that everyone know each other's names and perhaps an interesting tidbit or two about them.

- Sub-group with the same smaller group for discussion and prayer for a few months. Instead of rotating those subgroups each week, a three-month stretch allows relationships to form.
- Establish criteria for prayer that eliminates the "fake" prayer requests in favor of personal ones.
- Include ministry needs within the prayer time and suggest each group member should be engaged in serving others.
- Every few months plan a service project together to serve others and build more relational bridges.

Harmony is not complicated, but it does take some effort. As we build the relational bridge within our group, we look to Jesus as the model of who we should become. As we change to become more like him we open our hearts to people in need inside and outside of the community of Christ. A group striving for harmony should together ask, "Where are we and where do we want to go as a group?" Each group should choose their own adventure. We don't force the group to open up, serve others, do a deeper Bible study, or become close friends. But we lay the patterns out and ask, "Where should we focus?"

Is There an Order to the Patterns?

While groups can certainly start in any of the three patterns, they should quickly build the connecting pattern or the group will likely die. Whether it's a Bible study or a serving team, if the relational pattern isn't established, group members will find it easy to miss. This might explain why so many volunteer teams struggle with retaining members. A group should then build on that relational bridge the patterns of change and cultivate. Whether we are volunteering in a ministry or joining a group to grow spiritually, the group should help each member change. We should look more like Jesus after spending time in a group. Many groups risk stagnation once they help their members connect and change. I think they risk declining because they focus too much within their group. The appropriate outcropping of connecting and changing is a heart for outsiders. Cultivating a missional life is often the focus of a group at an advanced stage of spiritual maturity. There are three good reasons to pursue all three patterns:

1. If a group doesn't help each member connect, it will end quickly.
2. If a group doesn't help each member change, it will end within a year.
3. If a group doesn't help each member cultivate, it might last a long time but it will eventually become very dissatisfying.

Give It a Try

The patterns of simple small groups work in all sorts of settings. It works for serving teams, Sunday school classes, children's and student ministries, and, of course, small groups. At Southeast Christian Church we have a long history of classroom-based learning. Some churches call it Sunday school or adult Bible fellowships, but it commonly involves a teacher and a room of learners. For about two hundred years in England and North America it has been a well-used model of spiritual development in many churches.

However, some leaders at my church began to notice that the classes lacked a relational element. As a result people were coming in one door and within a week or two were heading out the other. That's when Brett DeYoung, one of the ministers, suggested round tables, a rather simple step toward a more relational space. Since many of the classes were actually the size of large small groups, why not enhance the space relationally? Rather than rows of seats, Brett recommended that the classrooms include round tables that give people a sense of connecting with a handful of other people. There was concern at first that not everyone would be excited about the change, but most were thrilled to have a place to put their cup of coffee and their Bible.

While the classrooms are still mostly teacher-driven, now we're encouraging people to connect with one another in a more intentional way. Some classes encourage their members to sit at the same tables for a few months and others allow them to rotate around. Some teachers include table discussion time in the lesson and others set aside prayer time for the tables. By trying something as simple as round tables, we helped an environment that was focused on the change pattern to include the connecting pattern.

Whether it's a classroom-based large group or a home-based small group that is more focused on change, including the relational pattern is essential to build trust and encourage openness. If a group gets there they can move further through the other two patterns.

Cultivate is often the most intimidating pattern to include, but it shouldn't be. My church adopted a couple of Habitat for Humanity houses in 2007. As a new team leader of a staff of people I began to reflect on how to build a deeper sense of connection with each other. That's when I took my own advice and thought we could incorporate the missional pattern. On a cold October morning we gathered in west Louisville to hang vinyl siding on a new home. None of us were veteran siding hangers so after a fifteen-minute instruction from Chuck, the site foreman, we climbed ladders and scaffolding and got to work. For the next several hours we turned a box into a home. We went with the purpose of serving, but in the process connected with each other. The days prior to the project we were all wondering if the timing was right. We were all very busy, the weather was turning colder, and we all had great reservations about our skills (or should

I say lack of skills?). Ironically, after the day of hard work some asked when we were going to do that again. Giving a day a few times a year may not change the world, but it will pry our eyes off ourselves for a moment and remind us that God loves a hurting world and we should too.

Are There More Patterns?

The identification of the three patterns has been a long process. The conversation has involved several churches, countless pastors from across the country, and many more small group leaders. Since the patterns are flexible, many different facets of church life fit within these three. Cultivate can be a melting pot for evangelism, service, and influence with people outside the faith. Change is all about maturity, growth, worship, and intimacy with God. Connecting is a broader and more contemporary word for fellowship and really about building relationships with those inside the faith.

The Sacred Group

People have often approached sacred places in hopes that God would comfort and encourage them and help them change. Throughout biblical times, the sanctuary (or temple) was the place people went to feel close to God. When God gave the Holy Spirit to the church, he didn't place him in a physical structure. He placed him within those who follow Christ. Paul describes us as God's temple:

> Don't you know that you yourselves are God's temple and that God's Spirit lives in you? If anyone destroys God's temple, God will destroy him; for God's temple is sacred, and you are that temple.
>
> 1 Corinthians 3:16–17

Do you not know that your body is a temple of the Holy Spirit, who is in you, whom you have received from God? You are not your own.

1 Corinthians 6:19

No longer is there a sacred location. God's presence does not uniquely dwell in an earthly place. Instead, when believers gather it becomes a sacred place. We don't need to go to a temple (or a church building) in which we are comforted, encouraged, and changed. We gather with fellow followers of Christ. Your group is just as sacred as the temple in Jerusalem was!

The Group Leader Challenge

If you are a group leader, you have a sacred opportunity. You can build a sacred experience (with the help of God) where members are connecting, changing, and cultivating. I have enormous respect for what you do. You have the ability to influence your people more than any small group minister can. As I wrote this I had you in mind. In my earliest days of group leadership I was often confused and frustrated. I didn't understand the biblical patterns of group life. When my group was struggling, I didn't know why, and when my group was going well I simply hoped it would keep going well. I wish I knew years ago what I know now. While we can't rewind the tape of life and redo some ridiculous mistakes, perhaps as we go forward we can find health and spiritual vibrancy in a dynamic small group.

Connecting, changing, and cultivating are not three silver bullets that solve all small group problems. But they are three helpful patterns of leading your group to a taste of that first-century revolutionary movement that was simply called "the Way."

May you enjoy a community that is connecting with one another, changing to be more like Jesus, and cultivating missional lives.

166

afterword

When Bill Search told me he was going to put some of his thoughts down in book form, I was excited for all of us. I have been a fan of Bill for some time and have benefited firsthand from his insights and experiences through conferences and leadership circles. The fact that he identifies himself as a former skeptic has always made him all the more credible in my eyes. Bill is not merely a philosopher or theorist; he lives in the trenches of group life every day, having trans- ferred concepts and ideas to the real world of ministry. He has asked the tough questions and like all of us has seen the validity and naiveté of early assumptions.

I really like this book. All of it, but there were three as- pects that particularly jumped out at me. Let me start with the obvious. I like the name, *Simple Small Groups*. I love seeing big ideas boiled down to their bottom lines so that the take-away is clear. In our attempts to be exhaustive and complete, our tendency is to gravitate toward the complex and abstract, not the simple and clear. People gravitate that way. Organizations do. And small group strategies certainly can. As a helpful practitioner, Bill threw away the conceptual white noise and provided us a resource that is clear and helpful because it is simple. Simplicity and clarity always go hand in hand. It makes me wonder if the people in our small groups would call them simple? The title of this book alone should cause us to take a second look.

The second thing I liked about this book is that it focused us toward the patterns of a healthy small group. Rather than get caught up in the pros or cons of a particular group nuance or strategy (the how), Bill has focused us toward the basics of any effective group experience (the what). He effectively focused us on the fundamentals, reminding us that if we try to do too many things with our groups, we may fail at doing anything well. He starts with "connecting" well with a group of people because he knows we can't ever grow into our fullest potential disconnected and isolated from other people. As a co-worker of mine has said, when we entered into a relationship with Christ, we were connected to his body, not just his head. Many discipleship strategies seem to suggest the opposite. Without having others graciously mirror for us where we are and encouraging us on to where we can be, we'll never fully "change" to Christ-likeness and "cultivate" the missional lives that God desires for all of us. Connecting, changing, and cultivating; I love the imagery and clarity of that pattern. Now for the personal heavy lifting. Do our ministries come close to reflecting this pattern?

Finally, I like Bill's call to harmonize the patterns. Rather than calling us to the illusiveness of balance, Bill reminds us that groups will have different needs at different times and so harmony of the three patterns should be the goal over balance. As my seminary professor Howard Hendricks has been known to say, "Balance is that moment in time we hit when we're swinging from one extreme to another." Harmony of the patterns, Bill rightly states, is what keeps groups healthy and produces a synergy that no one pattern could produce. Have we focused our groups on that kind of harmony and are they producing that kind of synergy?

Certain things are important to me when I read a book like this. Is the book based on truth? If the Scriptures speak on the subject, is it consistent with what the text has to say? Is the book clearly written? In other words, is its primary message easily understood? Last, is the information helpful? Is it arranged in such a way that it helps me think through the issues and challenges my assumptions? *Simple Small Groups* knocks it out of the park as that kind of book for me.

Bill Willits
Director of Group Life,
North Point Community Church
Coauthor, *Creating Community*

appendix 1

key scripture for connecting

The following sections of Scripture speak of the vision of connecting with others who love God. They also give practical advice on how to build and maintain healthy relationships.

> Then God said, "Let us make human beings in our image, to be like us. They will reign over the fish in the sea, the birds in the sky, the livestock, all the wild animals on the earth, and the small animals that scurry along the ground." So God created human beings in his own image. In the image of God he created them; male and female he created them.
>
> Genesis 1:26–27 NLT

God, who is Trinity, created us in his image. We have a need for community just as God does.

> Two people are better off than one, for they can help each other succeed. If one person falls, the other can reach out

and help. But someone who falls alone is in real trouble. Likewise, two people lying close together can keep each other warm. But how can one be warm alone? A person standing alone can be attacked and defeated, but two can stand back-to-back and conquer. Three are even better, for a triple-braided cord is not easily broken.

Ecclesiastes 4:9–12 NLT

We are better off with a community where we can help each other than in isolation.

All the believers devoted themselves to the apostles' teaching, and to fellowship, and to sharing in meals (including the Lord's Supper), and to prayer. A deep sense of awe came over them all, and the apostles performed many miraculous signs and wonders. And all the believers met together in one place and shared everything they had. They sold their property and possessions and shared the money with those in need. They worshiped together at the Temple each day, met in homes for the Lord's Supper, and shared their meals with great joy and generosity—all the while praising God and enjoying the goodwill of all the people. And each day the Lord added to their fellowship those who were being saved.

Acts 2:42–47 NLT

This historical account establishes the patterns of the early church.

Psalm 133. It is a tremendous thing when brothers and sisters live in harmony.

Proverbs 18:13. Listen, don't talk.

Proverbs 19:11. Overlook each other's flaws.

Matthew 5:21–24. Resentment and bitterness toward others has a negative impact on our worship.

Matthew 18:15–17. The classic teaching from Jesus on confronting and resolving hurts.

Luke 1:39–45, 56. God prepared an encouraging relationship for Mary as she was faced with the awesome responsibility as mother of the Savior.

John 15:12–17. Jesus tells his close followers that we must love each other.

John 17:20–21. Jesus prayed just before his arrest that his disciples—then and now—would be unified and through that we would be a testimony to the world.

Acts 4:32–35. The early group of believers was unified and shared with those in need.

Acts 16:40. Paul and Silas encouraged a house church.

Romans 12:4–5. We each have a part to play in the lives of others.

Romans 12:10, 13–16. Focus on others, share with them, and pursue peaceful living.

Romans 15:7. Just as God has brought us in just as we are, we should accept into community people just as they are.

1 Corinthians 13:5. If we love the people in our community we won't keep track of the things they do that bother us.

Galatians 5:13–15. We should love each other as much as we love ourselves. It is our sinful temptation to harm each other.

Galatians 6:2. Share in each other's struggles.

Ephesians 4:2–4. Since we are part of one body and share the Holy Spirit, we should make every effort to show grace to each other.

Ephesians 4:26–27. Anger is an enemy of community. It gives Satan a place to begin destroying unity.

Ephesians 4:29–32. Our words impact each other. We should choose words that encourage and build each other up.

Ephesians 5:21. The Christian community is not about who's in charge but about mutual submission.

Philippians 2:1–4. Consider the needs of others before your own. Work together.

Colossians 3:13–15. We will be hurt and offended in community. In order to live in peace we have to be prepared to forgive.

1 Thessalonians 4:18. We should encourage one another with Scripture.

Hebrews 10:25. It would seem it's a challenge to keep a group meeting together. People begin to neglect the spiritual gathering.

James 4:1–2. Many interpersonal problems in community are the result of petty jealousy.

James 4:11. We shouldn't use words that harm each other.

James 5:9. Don't complain about each other; it will affect our relationship with God.

1 John 4:20–21. If we love God we must love brothers and sisters in Christ.

appendix 2

key scripture for changing

The following Scripture demonstrates the vision and the practical how-to to help people change through a community.

> Now these are the gifts Christ gave to the church: the apostles, the prophets, the evangelists, and the pastors and teachers. Their responsibility is to equip God's people to do his work and build up the church, the body of Christ. This will continue until we all come to such unity in our faith and knowledge of God's Son that we will be mature in the Lord, measuring up to the full and complete standard of Christ.
>
> Then we will no longer be immature like children. We won't be tossed and blown about by every wind of new teaching. We will not be influenced when people try to trick us with lies so clever they sound like the truth. Instead, we will speak the truth in love, growing in every way more and more like Christ, who is the head of his body, the church. He makes the whole body fit together perfectly. As each part does its

own special work, it helps the other parts grow, so that the whole body is healthy and growing and full of love.

Ephesians 4:11–16 NLT

God gave spiritual gifts to the community so that we can help each other fully mature.

Let us think of ways to motivate one another to acts of love and good works.

Hebrews 10:24 NLT

We need each other for the encouragement to keep growing.

Exodus 18:13–26. Moses's father-in-law recommended a system of care and development for the people. It involved various levels of leadership and broke the nation down into groups of ten. It is often called the "Jethro Principle."

Proverbs 15:22. We make better decisions when we have people share their advice.

Proverbs 27:17. We help each other improve.

John 21:15–17. The proof that we truly love Jesus is shown through how we try to develop his followers.

Romans 12:6–8. We each have a spiritual gift that we should use to help others.

Romans 15:14. We should be willing and able to teach each other.

1 Corinthians 12:7–11. Paul clearly communicates that the whole purpose of spiritual gifts is to help others.

1 Corinthians 12:14–27. Paul's metaphor of a physical body points out how badly we need each other to function well.

Galatians 6:1. We should be close enough to notice if a brother or sister is falling into sin and then we ought to care enough to pursue them.

Colossians 3:16. We are to teach and admonish each other.

1 Thessalonians 5:12–15. Paul highlights the importance of leadership while encouraging a unified community that challenges each other to live like Christ.

2 Timothy 2:24. We shouldn't be prone to argue with one another but able to teach truth to each other.

2 Timothy 3:16–17. The Scriptures are the content of community that helps each person mature.

2 Timothy 4:2. We should challenge each other to move forward spiritually.

James 5:16. Even though God forgives us when we confess to him, he still wants us to confess to others.

James 5:19–20. We shouldn't give up on brothers or sisters who wander from Christ but through the community attempt to pull them back.

1 Peter 5:2–4. While this passage was instructional for elders, it also teaches about the call of shepherding and reminds us that God will reward the work we do for him.

Jude 20–21. Build each other up in the faith.

key scripture for cultivating

Jesus traveled through all the towns and villages of that area, teaching in the synagogues and announcing the Good News about the Kingdom. And he healed every kind of disease and illness. When he saw the crowds, he had compassion on them because they were confused and helpless, like sheep without a shepherd. He said to his disciples, "The harvest is great, but the workers are few. So pray to the Lord who is in charge of the harvest; ask him to send more workers into his fields."

Matthew 9:35–38 NLT

The heart of God wants everyone shepherded, not just people inside the family of God.

Therefore, go and make disciples of all the nations, baptizing them in the name of the Father and the Son and the Holy Spirit. Teach these new disciples to obey all the commands

I have given you. And be sure of this: I am with you always, even to the end of the age.

Matthew 28:19–20 NLT

Jesus' "Great Commission" involves evangelism, baptism, and education on the Christian life—it's a whole life development.

You have heard me teach things that have been confirmed by many reliable witnesses. Now teach these truths to other trustworthy people who will be able to pass them on to others.

2 Timothy 2:2 NLT

Growing in the faith isn't simply accumulating information. It's about passing faith on to others who will do the same.

Ezekiel 34:1–16. Ezekiel contrasts the good and bad shepherd. This passage is a warning to people who look after their own well-being and not the well-being of others.

Mark 3:14–15. When Jesus began his earthly ministry he started by choosing a small group who would carry on his mission. If the use of a community to impact the world was how Jesus did it, we ought to as well.

John 13:34–35. The way a community of believers who treat each other well bears evidence of Christ's work to those outside the faith.

Acts 2:46–47. A community dedicated to God is attractive to those outside the faith.

1 Corinthians 12:7. Every believer has a spiritual gift that has been given to help believers and unbelievers.

1 Corinthians 14:12. Most of this passage is about speaking in tongues. However, Paul teaches clearly that the point of spiritual gifts is to help others.

2 Corinthians 1:3–4. Because God has helped us in our troubles, we should help others in theirs.

Ephesians 4:11–13. God has given all sorts of different gifts to help the church grow. In particular, the gift of evangelism focuses on helping those outside of the Christian community.

James 2:14–17. Our faith is demonstrated through the care we show to those in need. A community of Christ followers is concerned about the physical needs of others.

1 Peter 3:9. Do not act like this world, which is driven by revenge. Instead, attempt to draw people to Christ through goodness and gentleness.

1 Peter 4:9–11. Everyone should use their gift to serve people inside and outside of our Christian communities.

notes

Introduction

1. Throughout this book I will use the term *community* primarily to refer to groups, small groups, house churches, and community groups. I will be the first to admit that there are many ways to experience community apart from a small group. For a marvelous treatment of the subject, see Joe Myers's books *The Search to Belong* and *Organic Community*. I will ask for grace in advance as I refer to community and small groups in the same manner.

2. See *Reveal: Where Are You?* by Greg Hawkins and Cally Parkinson. Their inside look at spiritual development at Willow Creek reveals some interesting data regarding spiritual development and group life.

3. Leyland showed great leadership and forced the team to study another exceptional team, the New York Yankees. http://www.nytimes.com/2006/10/15/sports/baseball/15leyland.html.

4. I quote Russ from Advanced Training at the Willow Creek Association in November of 2007. However, I have heard Russ say this more times than I can count!

Chapter 1

1. See Darrell Bock, *Acts* (Grand Rapids: Baker, 2007), 150–51 for a thorough discussion of the meal.

2. See Peter Bunton, *Cell Groups and House Churches: What History Teaches Us* (Ephrata, PA: House to House, 2001), 1–7.

3. http://www.intervarsity.org/aboutus/history.php.

183

Chapter 2

1. Ralph Waldo Emerson, "Essay VI—Friendship," *Essays: First Series,* 1841.
2. Throughout this book I will use stories from small groups. Many times I have changed names and certain details to protect the innocent (and the guilty).
3. According to the Nielsen Media Research the average American watches nearly five hours of TV a day. That's nearly thirty-five hours a week and over fifteen hundred hours a year! http://www.nielsenmedia. com/nc/portal/site/Public/menuitem.55dc65b4a7d5adff3f65936147a06 2a0/?vgnextoid=4156527aacccd010VgnVCM100000ac0a260aRCRD.
4. I am indebted to Joe Myers for this metaphor.

Chapter 3

1. I highly recommend you read Garry's book *Seeker Small Groups* (Grand Rapids: Zondervan, 2003). Even if you don't lead a Seeker group, the third section of his book contains excellent information on leading a good discussion.
2. Michael Watkins, *The First 90 Days* (Boston: Harvard Business School Press, 2003), 197.

Chapter 5

1. Hebrews 4:12–14; Psalm 119:5.
2. Bill Donahue, *Leading Life Changing Small Groups* (Grand Rapids: Zondervan, 1996).

Chapter 6

1. Alan Hirsch, *Forgotten Ways* (Grand Rapids: Brazos, 2006), 25.

Chapter 7

1. SHAPE, a curriculum from Brett Eastman's group, Lifetogether, and Willow Creek's Network series are pretty good. Both are published by Zondervan. Don't get hung up on identifying spiritual gifts. Focus as much effort on where your members could use their gifts.
2. Fortunately, I'm in good company. Dallas Willard writes of his disdain for the term in *Divine Conspiracy* (San Francisco: Harper, 1998). See page 10 for his more eloquent criticism of the term.

Chapter 8

1. As I have said before, what people mean by the term "Bible study" varies so much that I put quotation marks around it. For many, the act of Bible study is so cognitively focused that it fails to develop Christlikeness, which then begs the question, what is it?

Chapter 9

1. I'm indebted to Steve Gladen and Ron Wilbur at Saddleback Church for pushing me to better describe harmony and balance. Incidentally, in my humble opinion when my PDL friends talk about balancing the five purposes I think they mean what I mean by harmony. I've never heard them say you have to devote equal energy and time for the five purposes.

2. Bock, *Acts*, 154.

bibliography

Banks, Robert. *Paul's Idea of Community.* Peabody, MA: Hendrickson, 1994.

Bilezikian, Gilbert. *Community 101.* Grand Rapids: Zondervan, 1997.

Blackaby, Henry, and Claude King. *Experiencing God: How to Live the Full Adventure of Knowing and Doing the Will of God.* Nashville: Broadman and Holman, 1994.

Blanchard, Ken, and Phil Hodges. *The Servant Leader: Transforming Your Heart, Head, Hands and Habits.* Nashville: Thomas Nelson, 2003.

Bock, Darrell L. *Acts.* Grand Rapids: Baker, 2007.

Bonhoeffer, Dietrich. *Life Together.* San Francisco: Harper, 1954.

Bruce, A. B. *The Training of the Twelve.* Grand Rapids: Kregel, 1971.

Buckingham, Marcus, and Donald O. Clifton. *Now, Discover Your Strengths.* New York: Free Press, 2001.

Bunton, Peter. *Cell Groups and House Churches: What History Teaches Us.* Ephrata, PA: House to House, 2001.

Cloud, Henry, and John Townsend. *How People Grow: What the Bible Reveals about Personal Growth.* Grand Rapids: Zondervan, 2001.

———. *Making Small Groups Work.* Grand Rapids: Zondervan, 2003.

Coleman, Lyman. *The Serendipity Encyclopedia*. Littleton, CO: Serendipity House, 1997.

Collins, Jim. *Good to Great and the Social Sectors*. Boulder, CO: Jim Collins, 2005.

Dawn, Marva J. *Truly the Community: Romans 12 and How to Be the Church*. Grand Rapids: Eerdmans, 1992.

Deutschman, Alan. *Change or Die*. Los Angeles: Regan, 2007.

Donahue, Bill. *Leading Life-Changing Small Groups*. Grand Rapids: Zondervan, 1996.

Donahue, Bill, and Russ Robinson. *Building a Church of Small Groups*. Grand Rapids: Zondervan, 2001.

———. *The Seven Deadly Sins of a Small Group Ministry*. Grand Rapids: Zondervan, 2002.

———. *Walking the Small Group Tightrope*. Grand Rapids: Zondervan, 2003.

Downs, Tim, and Joy Downs. *Fight Fair: Winning at Conflict without Losing at Love*. Chicago: Moody, 2003.

Fischer, John. *12 Steps for the Recovering Pharisee (like me)*. Minneapolis: Bethany, 2000.

Frazee, Randy. *The Connecting Church*. Grand Rapids: Zondervan, 2001.

———. *Making Room for Life*. Grand Rapids: Zondervan, 2004.

Gladwell, Malcolm. *Blink: The Power of Thinking without Thinking*. New York: Little, Brown and Company, 2005.

Hawkins, Greg, and Cally Parkinson. *Reveal*. Barrington, IL: Willow Creek Resources, 2007.

Hirsch, Alan. *The Forgotten Ways*. Grand Rapids: Brazos Press, 2006.

Kempis, Thomas à. *The Imitation of Christ*. New York: Penguin Books, 1952.

Kotter, John P., and Dan S. Cohen. *The Heart of Change: Real-Life Stories of How People Change Their Organizations*. Boston: Harvard Business School Press, 2002.

Lawrenz, Mel. *Patterns*. Grand Rapids: Zondervan, 2003.

———. *Putting the Pieces Back Together: How Real Life and Real Faith Connect*. Grand Rapids: Zondervan, 2005.

Lebar, Lois E. *Education That Is Christian*. Wheaton, IL: Victor, 1995.

Lencioni, Patrick. *Death by Meeting*. San Francisco: Jossey-Bass, 2004.

———. *The Five Dysfunctions of a Team*. San Francisco: Jossey-Bass, 2002.

McCallum, Dennis, and Jessica Lowery. *Organic Disciplemaking*. Houston: Touch, 2006.

McKenna, Patrick J., and David H. Maister. *First Among Equals*. New York: Free Press, 2002.

McManners, John, ed. *The Oxford Illustrated History of Christianity*. Oxford: Oxford University Press, 1992.

McNeal, Reggie. *Practicing Greatness: 7 Disciplines of Extraordinary Spiritual Leaders*. San Francisco: Jossey-Bass, 2006.

———. *A Work of Heart: Understanding How God Shapes Spiritual Leaders*. San Francisco: Jossey-Bass, 2000.

Michelli, Joseph A. *The Starbucks Experience: 5 Principles for Turning Ordinary into Extraordinary*. New York: McGraw Hill, 2007.

Morrell, Margot, and Stephanie Capparell. *Shackleton's Way: Leadership Lessons from the Great Antarctic Explorer*. New York: Penguin Books, 2001.

Myers, Joseph. *Organic Community*. Grand Rapids: Baker, 2007.

———. *The Search to Belong: Rethinking Intimacy, Community and Small Groups*. Grand Rapids: Zondervan, 2003.

Nouwen, Henri J. M. *The Way of the Heart: Desert Spirituality and Contemporary Ministry*. San Francisco: Harper, 1981.

Ortberg, John. *Everybody's Normal Till You Get to Know Them*. Grand Rapids: Zondervan, 2003.

Palmer, Parker J. *To Know as We Are Known: Education as a Spiritual Journey*. San Francisco: Harper, 1993.

Plueddemann, Jim, and Carol Plueddemann. *Pilgrims in Progress: Growing through Groups*. Wheaton, IL: Harold Shaw, 1990.

Poole, Garry. *Seeker Small Groups*. Grand Rapids: Zondervan, 2003.

Quinn, Robert E. *Deep Change: Discovering the Leader Within*. San Francisco: Jossey-Bass, 1996.

Roberts, Bob Jr. *Transformation*. Grand Rapids: Zondervan, 2006.

Schwarz, Christian A. *Natural Church Development: A Guide to Eight Essential Qualities of Healthy Churches.* St. Charles, IL: ChurchSmart, 1996.

Stanley, Andy, and Bill Willits. *Creating Community.* Sisters, OR: Multnomah, 2004.

Stark, David, and Betty Veldman Weiland. *Growing People through Small Groups.* Minneapolis: Bethany House, 2004.

Tenney, Merrill. *New Testament Times.* Grand Rapids: Eerdmans, 1965.

Thrall, Bill, Bruce McNicol, and Ken McElrath. *The Ascent of a Leader.* San Francisco: Jossey-Bass, 1999.

Vanier, Jean. *Community and Growth.* New York: Paulist, 2003.

Watkins, Michael. *The First 90 Days: Critical Success Strategies for New Leaders at All Levels.* Boston: Harvard Business School Press, 2003.

Warren, Rick. *The Purpose Driven Life.* Grand Rapids: Zondervan, 2002.

Webb, Heather. *Small Group Leadership as Spiritual Direction: Practical Ways to Blend an Ancient Art into Your Contemporary Community.* Grand Rapids: Zondervan, 2005.

Wilhoit, James C., and John M. Dettoni. *Nurture That Is Christian.* Wheaton, IL: Victor, 1995.

Willard, Dallas. *The Divine Conspiracy: Rediscovering Our Hidden Life in God.* San Francisco: Harper, 1998.

Yancey, Philip. *Church: Why Bother?* Grand Rapids: Zondervan, 1998.

http://www.revealnow.com/attachments/smallGroupData.pdf

Bill Search is the team leader for Community Groups at Southeast Christian Church in Louisville, Kentucky, a church with an average weekly attendance of about 18,000. He has worked with the Willow Creek Association as a trainer and advisor for small groups for several years. Once a small group skeptic, Bill became a true believer in the power of community after his wife, Karyn, made him join a group. They now live in the Kentucky countryside with their three children, Maggie, Emma, and Jack. When not hanging out with his beautiful wife or chasing his kids around the yard, he's haunting his local Starbucks. His oddest hobby is collecting military chaplain communion sets and equipment. Visit his website at www.simplesmallgroups.com.